WITHDRÁWN

Adrian Henri
Total Artist

Occasional Papers

Cabinet of Curiosities, Adrian Henri's house, Liverpool

Foreword
Adrian Henri's *Musées imaginaires*
Catherine Marcangeli

Adrian Henri (1932–2000) came to prominence as a writer alongside poets
Roger McGough and Brian Patten in the groundbreaking Penguin anthology
The Mersey Sound (1967), one of the best-selling poetry books of all time.
His live poetry readings, and his ability to juxtapose everyday or pop images
with highbrow cultural references, shaped several generations' perceptions
of what poetry could be, and could be about. These questions are broached in
Henri's 'Notes on Painting and Poetry', reprinted here in full for the first
time since 1968.[1]

Henri trained as a painter at King's College, Newcastle, under Roger de
Grey, Victor Pasmore and Richard Hamilton. He moved back to Liverpool in 1956,
later teaching at the Art College there. His early Pop Art sensibility translated
into urban imagery, collages and hyperrealist paintings of meat against a
clinical white background. He was also a pioneer of happenings in Britain,
setting up the first event in Liverpool in 1962,[2] collaborating with Wendy and
Bill Harpe, Robert Conybear (Rob Con) and Lol Coxhill into the 1970s, and
corresponding with artists involved in performance including Allan Kaprow,
Yoko Ono and Mark Boyle. Henri's practice of collage and his concurrent
exploration of happenings as an ultimate form of assemblage are evoked in
my essay, and the context and repercussions of Henri's landmark publication
Environments and Happenings are reassessed by Antony Hudek.

Performance was central to Henri's work, both as a visual artist and as
a poet. He gave numerous poetry readings throughout his career and, in the
1960s and 1970s, fronted the poetry and rock group The Liverpool Scene, signed
by RCA. Their debut album was produced by John Peel, who dubbed Henri 'one
of the great non-singers of our time'. In 1969, the band performed at the Isle of
Wight Festival, supported Led Zeppelin and toured America. The innovations
and legacy of Henri's work with music are examined in Bryan Biggs' essay.

In 'Notes on Painting and Poetry', Henri insists that he found 'no difficulty
(other than shortage of time)'[3] in being a painter, poet, organiser of happenings,
teacher and touring musician. This versatility is paired with an open-minded
curiosity for and delight in other artists' work. Far from shying away from what
Harold Bloom termed the 'anxiety of influence',[4] he enthusiastically summoned
into his own work a cast of artists, writers and musicians. Through quotation,
reference, variations or versions, homage or parody, a dialogue with the past
and the present was thus ongoing. This claiming of tradition chimed with
T.S. Eliot's conviction that a historical sense was indispensible to anyone
wishing to be a poet beyond the age of twenty-five:

the historical sense involves a perception, not only of the pastness of the past, but of its presence; the historical sense compels a man to write not merely with his own generation in his bones, but with a feeling that the whole of the literature of Europe from Homer and within it the whole of the literature of his own country has a simultaneous existence and composes a simultaneous order. This historical sense (...) makes a writer most acutely conscious of his place in time, of his contemporaneity.[5]

Eliot's 'Tradition and the Individual Talent' had a great impact on Henri, for whom this historical sense was constitutive – not a matter of dry academic erudition, but rather like an album of favourites, old and new, constantly playing in the background and being added to. An early poem by Henri published in *The Mersey Sound* takes Eliot's imperatives to tongue-in-cheek extremes. Titled 'Me', it answers an initial question – 'If you weren't you, who would you like to be?' – with a list that includes jazz musicians, pop singers and classical composers, medieval, Dada and contemporary artists, romantic and modernist poets, Beat writers, filmmakers, actors, friends and heroes. The names are not arranged by categories based on their disciplines, fame or place in the canon. 'Me' is a manifesto, stressing the presentness of the past through surprising juxtapositions, suggesting that one can, must, admire both Claude Debussy and The Clayton Squares, Kurt Schwitters and Matthias Grünewald.[6]

    The poem reads like an apparently arbitrary, unpunctuated list, yet when it is read out loud, one becomes aware that the necessities of rhythm dictate the order in which the names are reeled off. For this is also a formal experiment in scansion: at the sixth stanza, the beat changes from regular stressed/unstressed syllables to a more syncopated rhythm. During live readings, Henri often marked a pause after 'Manfred Mann' to announce knowingly 'change of rhythm':[7]

Salvatore Giuliano
Andy Warhol Paul Cézanne
Kafka Camus Ensor Rothko
Jacques Prévert and Manfred Mann

Marx Dostoievsky
Bakunin Ray Bradbury
Miles Davis Trotsky
Stravinsky and Poe[8]

Henri was 'interested in how far poetry can be pushed in different directions and still remain poetry. Can a poem be a letter? A news item? A cut-up of disparate material? A concrete typographic statement that couldn't be read out?'[9] He could have added: can it be a list of names, a freewheeling sequence of almost abstract sounds, whose poetic status is warranted by its musicality? Depending on each reader's background and interests, different names would bring to mind different images or sounds in quick succession, producing kaleidoscopic echoes.

In *The Entry of Christ into Liverpool in 1964* (Fig. 37), Henri similarly assembles a cast of friends and heroes, real and imaginary. The painting is a variation on James Ensor's *Entry of Christ into Brussels in 1889* (1888). In Henri's version, Ensor is Christ, and in front of him, Alfred Jarry is riding a bicycle. In the front row stands the rotund figure of Père Ubu, the absurd and autocratic protagonist of some of Jarry's best-known plays. Also present are William Burroughs, Charles Mingus and Charlie Parker, as well as members of Liverpool's 1960s bohemia, such as Philip Jones Griffiths (a school friend of Henri's and later a respected Magnum war photographer), Pete Brown (Beat jazz-poet who took part in Henri's early events, and later wrote lyrics for the band Cream), painters Don McKinlay and Sam Walsh, George Melly (jazz singer, raconteur and Henri's first art patron), Mike Evans (musician-poet, later member of The Liverpool Scene) and poets Patten and McGough. The characters face us, static and silent, the frontality of the composition giving the painting a strange solemnity.

In the corresponding poem written shortly after the painting was completed, the description of the scene is anything but static: the familiar linearity of sentences is, on the contrary, disrupted by repetitions and fragmentations, variations in typography, as snippets of a feverish cityscape convey a sense of hallucinatory oppression. When performed to music with The Liverpool Scene, the poem is more haunting still, its rhythm the stop-go heartbeat of a city gasping for breath, shrill trumpet and saxophone echoing as Guinness signs flash overhead in stammering bursts:

GUIN
GUINN
GUINNESS IS
white bird dying unnoticed in a corner
splattered feathers
blood running merged with the neonsigns
in a puddle
GUINNESS   IS   GOOD
GUINNESS   IS   GOOD   FOR
Masks   Masks   Masks   Masks   Masks
GUINNESS IS GOOD FOR YOU[10]

'The Entry of Christ' is firmly located in Liverpool, and street names give a specificity to the scene, lending it an increased sense of reality which further jars with the fantastical spectacle. Henri often relocated scenes or characters to his home city: in one poem, Marcel Proust dunks madeleine butties in his tea at the local Kardomah cafe. Henri's play *The Big Feller*, an adaptation of Jarry's *Ubu Roi*, is also set in 1960s Liverpool, and comically pits Ubu's stilted language against colourful Scouse idioms. In several paintings too, Père Ubu walks the streets of Liverpool.

This recurrent relocation and appropriation process is not a form of proudly claimed provincialism. More interestingly, it is as though Henri were creating a parallel city where characters and artists he liked and admired convened and mingled with the locals, a mental city in which his imaginary museum flourished. When André Malraux developed the concept of the *Musée imaginaire*, he was referring to the mass of images we carry with us, particularly artworks we know thanks to photographs.[11] His museum had no walls, no 'Italian Quattrocento' nor 'Dutch Genre Painting' wings: Malraux did away with chronology and traditional pedagogy to juxtapose images in his open-ended survey of man's varied creations. There is something quite deliberate, editorial or curatorial, about his juxtapositions, yet his imaginary museum very much remains a fluctuating mental landscape where works respond to, and are fed or modified by, each other.

Henri's own version of the imaginary museum has affinities to the 18th-century cabinet of curiosities, the Surrealists' chance encounter of umbrella and sewing machine, Eliot's vision of tradition, Malraux's album of persistent images and Hamilton's high-low continuum. It is a juxtaposition and a palimpsest, a sum and a network, a political act of communication, the invitation of a *passeur* to inhabit 'the gap between art and life'.[12]

1   First published in *Tonight at Noon* (London: Rapp & Whiting, 1968).

2   *City*, part of the Merseyside Arts Festival, Hope Hall, Liverpool.

3   Henri, 'Notes on Painting and Poetry', 109 in the present volume.

4   Harold Bloom, *The Anxiety of Influence* (New York: Oxford University Press, 1973).

5   T.S. Eliot, 'Tradition and the Individual Talent' (1919), in *The Sacred Wood: Essays on Poetry and Criticism* (New York: Alfred A. Knopf, 1921).

6   As a student, Henri was captivated by Hamilton's lectures on Schwitters, yet he elected to write an extended essay on Grünewald's early 16th-century Isenheim Altarpiece (Henri's student notebook, Adrian Henri Archive, Estate of Adrian Henri, Liverpool).

7   In doing so, Henri was directly referring to the world of jazz, particularly Charles Mingus and John Coltrane: whereas pop music usually followed a $^4/_4$ rhythm, the jazz musicians Henri most admired often started with a standard theme, but then went on to deconstruct it, introducing syncopations or variations.

8   'Me', in *The Mersey Sound* (London: Penguin, 1967), 27.

9   Henri, 'Notes on Painting and Poetry', 111 in the present volume.

10 'The Entry of Christ into Liverpool' in *The Mersey Sound*, revised edition (London: Penguin, 1974), 46. The poem was recorded by The Liverpool Scene, track 4 of *Bread on the Night* (RCA, 1969), and reissued on *The Amazing Adventures of the Liverpool Scene* (Cherry Red Records, 2009).

11 André Malraux, *Le Musée imaginaire* (Paris: Gallimard, 1965).

12 Henri often quoted Robert Rauschenberg's dictum that the artist should work in the gap between art and life.

In the Top 20:
Selected Poems

Adrian Henri

Tonight at Noon

(for Charles Mingus and The Clayton Squares)

Tonight at noon
Supermarkets will advertise 3d EXTRA on everything
Tonight at noon
Children from happy families will be sent to live in a home
Elephants will tell each other human jokes
America will declare peace on Russia
World War I generals will sell poppies in the streets on November 11th
The first daffodils of autumn will appear
When the leaves fall upwards to the trees

Tonight at noon
Pigeons will hunt cats through city backyards
Hitler will tell us to fight on the beaches and on the landing fields
A tunnel full of water will be built under Liverpool
Pigs will be sighted flying in formation over Woolton
and Nelson will not only get his eye back but his arm as well
White Americans will demonstrate for equal rights
in front of the Black House
And the Monster has just created Dr Frankenstein

Girls in bikinis are moonbathing
Folksongs are being sung by real folk
Art galleries are closed to people over 21
Poets get their poems in the Top 20
Politicians are elected to insane asylums
There's jobs for everyone and nobody wants them
In back alleys everywhere teenage lovers are kissing
in broad daylight

In forgotten graveyards the dead will quietly bury the living
and
You will tell me you love me
Tonight at noon.

I Want to Paint

Part One

I want to paint
2000 dead birds crucified on a background of night
Thoughts that lie too deep for tears
Thoughts that lie too deep for queers
Thoughts that move at 186,000 miles/second
The Entry of Christ into Liverpool in 1966
The Installation of Roger McGough to the Chair of Poetry at Oxford
Francis Bacon making the President's Speech at the Royal Academy Dinner

I want to paint
50 life-sized nudes of Marianne Faithfull
(all of them painted from life)
Welsh Maids by Welsh Waterfalls
Heather Holden as Our Lady of Haslingden
A painting as big as Piccadilly full of neon signs buses
Christmas decorations and beautiful girls with dark blonde hair shading their faces

I want to paint
The assassination of the entire Royal Family
Enormous pictures of every pavingstone in Canning Street
The Beatles composing a new National Anthem
Brian Patten writing poems with a flamethrower on disused ferryboats
A new cathedral 50 miles high made entirely of pramwheels
An empty Woodbine packet covered in kisses
I want to paint
A picture made from the tears of dirty-faced children in Chatham Street

I want to paint
I LOVE YOU across the steps of St George's Hall
I want to paint
       pictures.

Part Two

I want to paint
The Simultaneous and Historical Faces of Death
10,000 shocking pink hearts with your name on
The phantom negro postmen who bring me money in my dreams
The first plastic daffodil of spring pushing its way
through the OMO packets in the supermarket
The portrait of every 6th-form schoolgirl in the country
A full-scale map of the world with YOU at the centre
An enormous lily-of-the-valley with every flower on a separate canvas

Lifesize jellybabies shaped like Hayley Mills
A black-and-red flag flying over Parliament
I want to paint
Every car crash on all the motorways of England
Père Ubu drunk at 11 o'clock at night in Lime Street
A SYSTEMATIC DERANGEMENT OF ALL THE SENSES
in black running letters 50 miles high over Liverpool
I want to paint
Pictures that children can play hopscotch on
Pictures that can be used as evidence at murder trials
Pictures that can be used to advertise cornflakes
Pictures that can be used to frighten naughty children
Pictures worth their weight in money
Pictures that tramps can live in
Pictures that children would find in their stockings on Christmas morning
Pictures that teenage lovers can send each other
I want to paint
                pictures.

Mrs Albion, You've Got a Lovely Daughter
(for Allen Ginsberg)

Albion's most lovely daughter sat on the banks of the Mersey
   dangling her landing stage in the water.

The daughters of Albion
   arriving by underground at Central Station
   eating hot ecclescakes at the Pierhead
   writing 'Billy Blake is Fab' on a wall in Mathew Street

   taking off their navyblue schooldrawers and
   putting on nylon panties ready for the night

The dauthers of Albion
   see the moonlight beating down on them in Bebington
   throw away their chewinggum ready for the goodnight kiss
sleep in the dinnertime sunlight with old men
   looking up their skirts in St Johns Gardens
comb their darkblonde hair in suburban bedrooms
powder their delicate little nipples/wondering if tonight will
   be the night
their bodies pressed into dresses or sweaters
lavender at The Cavern or pink at The Sink

The daughters of Albion wondering how to explain why they
   didn't go home

The daughters of Albion
   taking the dawn ferry to tomorrow
   worrying about what happened
   worrying about what hasn't happened
   lacing up blue sneakers over brown ankles
   fastening up brown stockings to blue suspenderbelts

Beautiful boys with bright red guitars
in the spaces between the stars

Reelin' an' a-rockin'
Wishin' an' a-hopin'
Kissin' an' a-prayin'
Lovin' an' a-layin'

Mrs Albion, you've got a lovely daughter.

Love Is...

Love is feeling cold in the back of vans
Love is a fanclub with only two fans
Love is walking holding paintstained hands
Love is

Love is fish and chips on winter nights
Love is blankets full of strange delights
Love is when you don't put out the light
Love is

Love is the presents in Christmas shops
Love is when you're feeling Top of the Pops
Love is what happens when the music stops
Love is

Love is white panties lying all forlorn
Love is a pink nightdress still slightly warm
Love is when you have to leave at dawn
Love is

Love is you and love is me
Love is a prison and love is free
Love's what's there when you're away from me
Love is...

Me

if you weren't you, who would you like to be?

Paul McCartney Gustav Mahler
Alfred Jarry John Coltrane
Charlie Mingus Claude Debussy
Wordsworth Monet Bach and Blake

Charlie Parker Pierre Bonnard
Leonardo Bessie Smith
Fidel Castro Jackson Pollock
Gaudí Milton Munch and Berg

Béla Bartók Henri Rousseau
Rauschenberg and Jasper Johns
Lukas Cranach Shostakovich
Kropotkin Ringo George and John

William Burroughs Francis Bacon
Dylan Thomas Luther King
H.P. Lovecraft T.S. Eliot
D.H. Lawrence Roland Kirk

Salvatore Giuliano
Andy Warhol Paul Cézanne
Kafka Camus Ensor Rothko
Jacques Prévert and Manfred Mann

Marx Dostoievsky
Bakunin Ray Bradbury
Miles Davis Trotsky
Stravinsky and Poe

Danilo Dolci Napoleon Solo
St John of the Cross and
The Marquis de Sade

Charles Rennie Mackintosh
Rimbaud Claes Oldenburg
Adrian Mitchell and Marcel Duchamp

James Joyce and Hemingway
Hitchcock and Buñuel
Donald McKinlay Thelonious Monk

Alfred, Lord Tennyson
Matthias Grünewald
Philip Jones Griffiths and Roger McGough

Guillaume Apollinaire
Cannonball Adderley
René Magritte
Hieronymus Bosch

Stéphane Mallarmé and Alfred de Vigny
Ernst Mayakovsky and Nicolas de Staël
Hindemith Mick Jagger Dürer and Schwitters
García Lorca
        and
           last of all
             me.

Batpoem
(for Bob Kane and The Almost Blues)

Take me back to Gotham City
      Batman
Take me where the girls are pretty
      Batman
All those damsels in distress
Half-undressed or even less
The BatPill makes 'em all say Yes
      Batman

Help us out in Vietnam
      Batman
Help us drop that BatNapalm
      Batman
Help us bomb those jungle towns
Spreading pain and death around
Coke 'n' Candy wins them round
      Batman

Help us smash the Vietcong
      Batman
Help us show them that they're wrong
      Batman
Help us spread democracy
Get them high on LSD
Make them just like you and me
      Batman

Show me what I have to do
      Batman
'Cause I want to be like you
      Batman

Flash your Batsign over Lime Street
Batmobiles down every crime street
Happy Batday that's when I'll meet
      Batman

Plates

City

Henri's early work is predominantly urban in inspiration and iconography. He urged poets and artists to embrace the new images from advertising, television and popular culture, and to make full use of what he termed 'polythenescapes', of the 'pattern qualities' of logos, zebra crossings, neon signs, traffic lights, lines and words painted on roads. This contemporary bombardment of signs and messages was explored in *City* (1962), the first happening staged in Britain.

Henri also exposed the darker sides of cityscapes – racist graffiti scrawled across walls, birds 'found screaming white splattered against windscreens' or, as in his later happenings, whole areas destroyed by planners.

Fig. 1 *Box*, c. 1962, mixed media assemblage, 41 × 31 cm

Above: **Fig. 2** *Small Fairground Image I*, 1961, mixed media on board, 61 × 45 cm
Opposite: **Fig. 3** *Piccadilly Painting II*, 1964, oil and collage on board, 183 × 117 cm

CITY EVENT: AN INTRODUCTION

An 'event' is a sort of theatrical or dramatic ritual happening
aimed at working directly on the consciousness of thos experiencing
it.   It uses mime, dance, poetry, painting and music mixed in
varying proportions.   The audience are contained within an
environment, which is also part of the action.

The 'events' so far organized have taken place in New York(this
one is, as far as we know, the first to take place in England).
They have usually been produced by painters (although basically
theatrical) and small art galleries are often used.   Intimacy
of setting is essential.   The painters who have been involved
in 'events' have been of the new school of 'Assemblage' painters
_____ Allan Kaprow, Jim Dine, Claes Oldenberg, Robert Rauschenberg.
These artists, as a reaction against the 'pure' action-painting of
the post-war New York school, have returned to the earlier Dada and
Surrealist idea of using intrinsically worthless junk as material
for painting and sculpture.   Thus painting and sculpture tend to
come together, and from this attitude it is a short step to using
music, vocal imagery and live actors in a 3-dimensional 'canvas'.
The great pre-war Surrealist exhibitions were the direct ancestors
of these 'events'.

Recent developments in Dance and Drama in U.S.A. have been
profoundly affected by this 'integration of the arts' idea.   Indeed,
the nearest thing to an 'event' which has been seen in England is
Jack Gelber's play 'The Connection'.

The two specifically 20th Century art-forms jazz and the cinema, are
both products of a team, and are to a greater or lesser extent
improvisatory or 'fluid' in conception.   A jazz attitude is at the
back of these 'events' or 'happenings' which are in effect what
musicians call 'head-arrangements (i.e. not written out but largely
pre-determined) which allow for existential reactions to the actual
situation as it happens.

The poetry is not concerned with narrative but is rather an attempt to
project emotional 'herd' atmosphere through impressionistic tactile
imagery adapted from the King-size polythenescape of which we in the city
are all a part —— (i.e. audiotactilism).

The 'event' is one of the new cross-fertilizations(like Jazz Canto or
Poetry & Jazz) which are enriching the old fixed art-forms, movements
which are largely 'subterranean', independent and unknown to modern
literary, artistic and theatrical Establishment.

This 'event' is presented by arrangement with the Merseyside Arts Festival
Committee.

Adrian Henri

Roger Mc Gough

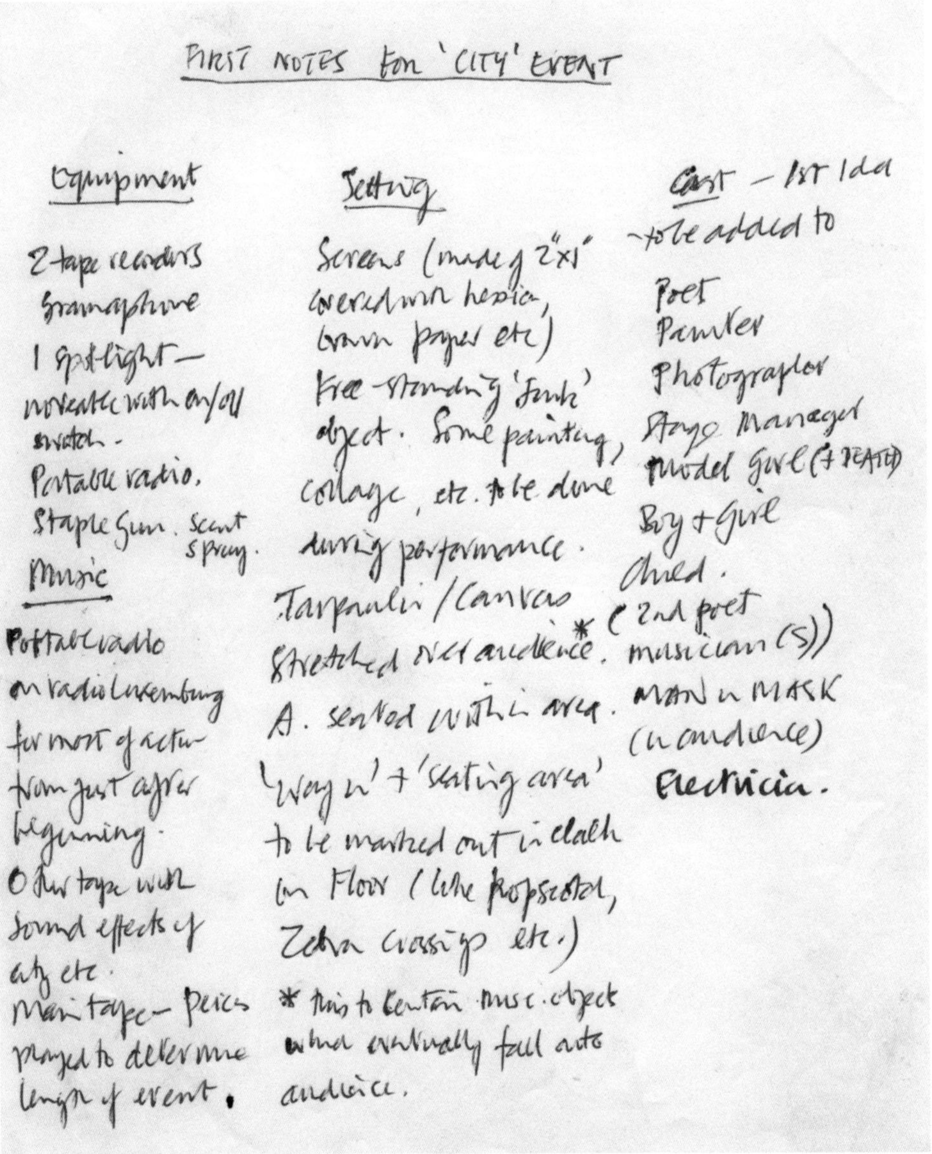

FIRST NOTES FOR 'CITY' EVENT

Equipment	Setting	Cast – 1st Idea
		– to be added to
2 tape recorders	Screens (made of 2"x1"	Poet
Gramaphone	covered with hessian,	Painter
1 spotlight –	brown paper etc)	Photographer
moveable with on/off	Free-standing 'Junk'	Stage Manager
switch.	object. Some painting,	Model girl (? TREATED)
Portable radio.	collage, etc. to be done	Boy + Girl
Staple Gun. Scent	during performance.	Child.
spray.	Tarpaulin / Canvas	(2nd poet
Music	stretched over audience. ∗	musician (s))
Portable radio	A. seated within area.	MAN in MASK
on Radio Luxembourg	'Way in' + 'seating area'	(in audience)
for most of action	to be marked out in chalk	Electrician.
from just after	on Floor (like Hopscotch,	
beginning.	Zebra crossing etc.)	
Other tape with		
sound effects of	∗ this to contain music object	
city etc.	which eventually fall onto	
Main tape – pieces	audience.	
played to determine		
length of event.		

Left: **Fig. 4** Adrian Henri, Roger McGough, *City Event: An Introduction*
(second version), Manchester College of Art, December 1962
Above: **Fig. 5** *First Notes for 'City' Event*, Hope Hall, Liverpool, August 1962

Living art—but it's so confusing

THE audience at a city's festival of arts sat waiting for the grand finale. Then it came—right on their heads !

Soap flakes, bottle tops, sweets and advertising literature showered down on them. This, said the organisers, was living art.

It happened last night in Liverpool's Everyman's Theatre Club.

As the shower came down, tape recordings of popular T V advertising jingles blared out, while an attractive girl wearing a provocative black sweater, slacks and a mask danced between the seats.

Enjoyed it

Said Mr. Roger McGough, one of the organisers: "The whole idea of this was impact. The walls were covered, quite purposely, in advertising material and the things you find scrawled on walls."

Mr. Michael Weinblatt, a ladies hairdresser, aged 23, went into greater detail, "This event is the first of its kind in Europe.

"Greenwich Village in New York has had them—but never has it been attempted here. The idea was to show exactly how little the average person sees of modern life."

As the 60 invited guests came out, covered in soapflakes, chewing sweets and swapping bottle tops, they appeared to have enjoyed it.

The advertising material on the tape recording was about as god as the advertising material on the walls. Both were, to the average human being, senseless.

But that, according to the organisers, was the idea.

Said Mr. Adrian Henri, one of the original thinkers behind this grand finale: "The poetry of advertising, the drums we used and the bits of odd music, are not concerned with narrative, but rather an attempt to project emotional "herd" atmosphere   **D. S.**

Fig. 6 Newspaper review of *City* event, Hope Hall, Liverpool, August 1962

Top: **Fig. 7** Set for *City* event, Merseyside Arts Festival, Hope Hall, Liverpool, August 1962
Bottom: **Fig. 8** Adrian Henri (left), Roger McGough (middle) and Pete Brown (right)

Fig. 9 *24 Collages, Liverpool 8 Spring Collage No. 5 (for PGW & FB)*, 1965, collage
and paint on paper, 32 × 26 cm

Fig. 10 *Big Liverpool 8 Murder Painting*, 1963, mixed media on board, 152.5 × 122 cm

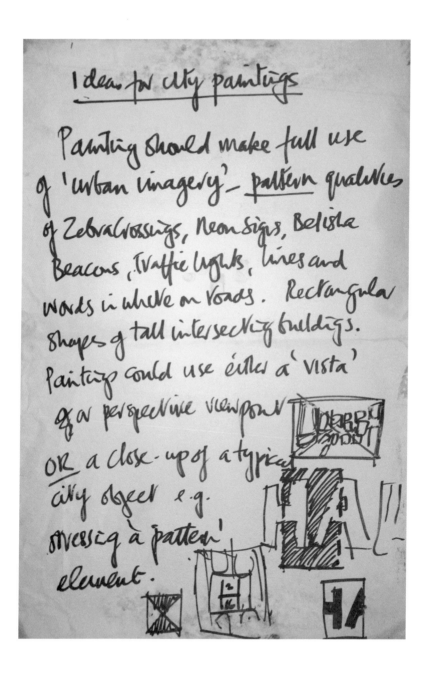

Ideas for city paintings

Painting should make full use of 'urban imagery' — pattern qualities of Zebra Crossings, Neon signs, Belisha Beacons, Traffic lights, lines and words in white on roads. Rectangular shapes of tall intersecting buildings. Paintings could use either a 'vista' or a perspective viewpoint OR a close-up of a typical city object e.g. stressing a 'pattern' element.

Top: **Fig. 11** *Ideas for city paintings*, c. 1961, ink on paper
Right: **Fig. 12** *Small Fairground Image 3*, 1961, mixed media on board, 61 × 45 cm

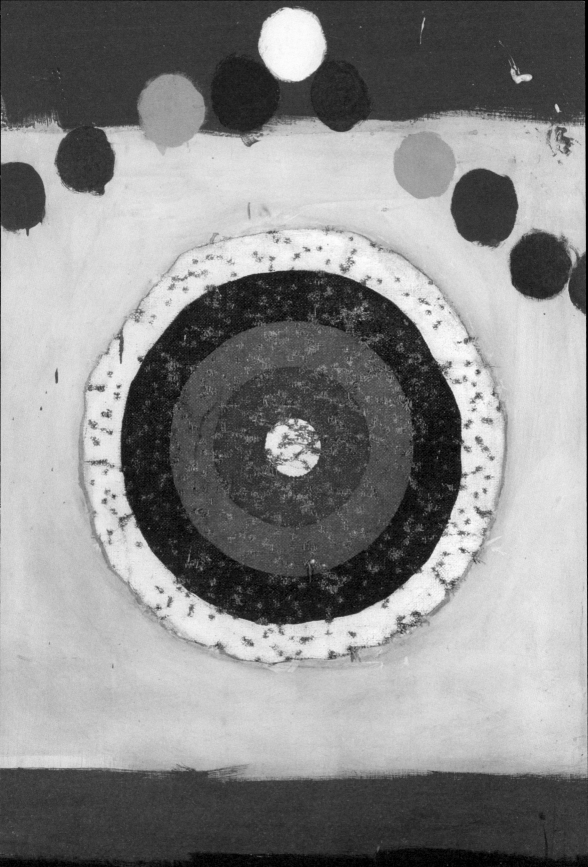

Fig. 13 *Liverpool 8 Four Seasons Painting*, 1964, mixed media on board,
each panel 183 × 76 cm

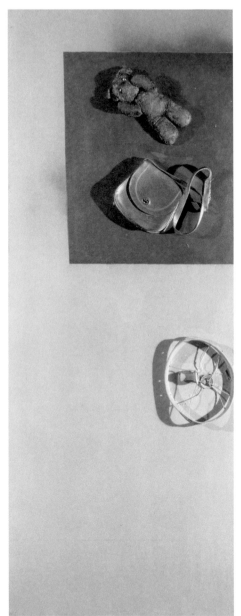

31

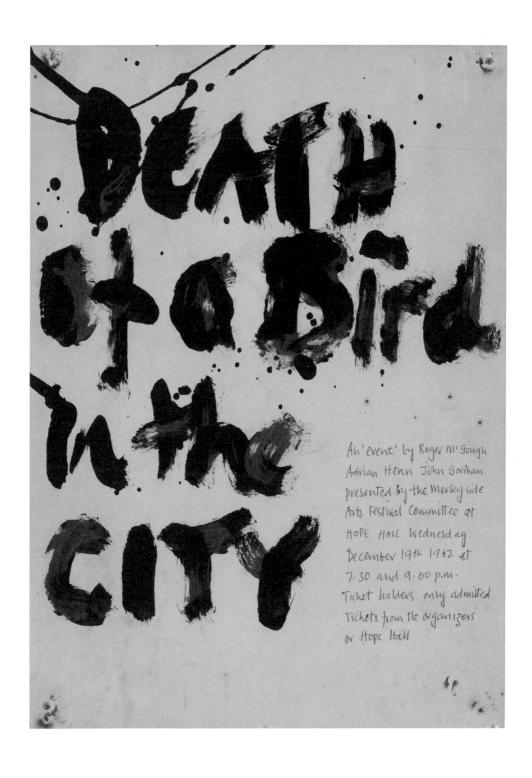

Fig. 14 Poster for *Death of a Bird in the City* event presented on 19 December 1962
by the Merseyside Arts Festival Committee, Hope Hall, Liverpool, 38 × 28 cm

Fig. 15 *Bird of Prey*, 1960, oil on board, 120 × 120 cm

Fig. 16 *Painting 1*, 1972, acrylic on board, 122 × 213.5 cm

34

DEAR MR. FANTASY ....

In the 1930's the Surrealists worked to introduce the domain of the
marvellous into everyday life. Flaver-headed women walked the streets
of London. Salvador Dali planned for giant loaves of bread to be found
in city centres. This was at a time of intense concern with political
and social issues. In 1968 the revolutionary French students painted
Andre Breton's slogan ALL POWER TO THE IMAGINATION across the barricades
of Nanterre.

This term I should like to examine the possibility of making dreams live,
enriching everyday life through fantasy. DREAMS IN THE STREET, a lecture
on October 23rd will examine the ways in which artists this century have
taken art into the streets and out of the galleries. NOVEMBER DREAMS
will be a week's project from 28th October culminating in a one-day event
on 2nd November at Great Georges Project, Liverpool, as part of their
'Building Sight' programme. An observation-window made to watch progress
of the rebuilding of the interior used as the focus of events on the site
inside the building, to be seen through the window. The activity I
envisage would be a communal one, made from co-ordinated individual
images under the 'umberella' title. The title refers to the changes of
seasons, autumn into winter, season of hallowe'en and bonfires, Michaelmas
and All Souls day.

Finally, I should like to examine the role of myth and fantasy in the
cinema as part of the end-of-term film festival.

Students wishing to participate in the 'November Dreams/Great Georges'
project should contact me within the next week.

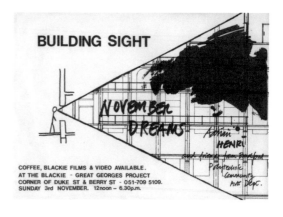

Top: **Fig. 17** *'Dear Mr Fantasy'*, proposal for
November Dreams, Building Sight event, Bradford
Polytechnic Community Arts Department, 1974
Bottom: **Fig. 18** Leaflet for *November Dreams,
Building Sight* event at The Blackie, Great Georges
Project, Liverpool, 2–3 November 1974, 21 × 29.5 cm
Opposite: **Fig. 19** Photographs of *November
Dreams, Building Sight* event at The Blackie, Great
Georges Project, Liverpool, 2–3 November 1974

BUILDING SIGHT

NOVEMBER DREAMS

Adrian HENRI
and friends from Bradford
Polytechnic Community
Arts Dept.

COFFEE, BLACKIE FILMS & VIDEO AVAILABLE.
AT THE BLACKIE - GREAT GEORGES PROJECT
CORNER OF DUKE ST & BERRY ST - 051-709 5109.
SUNDAY 3rd NOVEMBER. 12noon – 6.30p.m.

SIX MEMORIALS

A 'Gift to the City' for Wendy Harpe.

Action

A white line to be drawn round a paving-stone on the following sites,
using spraypaint, scotch tape or whatever (on places where there are
no paving-stones, a rectangle the size of an average one to be marked
out).

A wreath of appropriate flowers to be placed within the rectangle.

This to be done on the following sites :

1. The old 'Paddy's Market'. *(Cazneau St.)*

2. The entrance to the Old St. John's Market.

3. Harry's chip-shop, Falkner Street.
   Fat Johnny's Club, Upper Canning St.
4. ~~The boarding-place for the New Brighton ferry.~~   *(Alteration 6 · viii · 71)*

5. The Basnett Bar, Basnett Street.

6. The ticket-barrier for the Manchester line, Central Station.

NOTES

1. The research for the exact location of some of these to be part
   of the piece.

2. Appropriate clothes to be worn for the ceremony.

3. Appropriate words to be said if thought fitting.
   Poems, extracts from the burial service, or new words, e.g.

        "Ashes to Ashes
         Dust to Dust
         If the bombs don't get you
         The Planners must"

Although silence might be more effective.

                                        Adrian Henri   2.8.71.

Fig. 20 Script for *Six Memorials, A Gift to the City (for Wendy Harpe)* by
Adrian Henri for The Blackie, Great Georges Project, Liverpool, August 1971

Art is not an end in itself but a means to function thoroughly and
passionately in a world that has a lot more than paint in it.
Robert Rauschenberg

Fig. 21 Documentation of Adrian Henri's *Six Memorials, A Gift to the City
(for Wendy Harpe)*, The Blackie, Great Georges Project, Liverpool, August 1971,
in *Gift to a City*, calendar, 1973, 41 × 33 cm

Love

Henri is best known as a writer of love poetry, charting chance encounters, everyday enchantments, false starts and reluctant separations. He rarely painted portraits, but used hearts, initials or collages of everyday objects to indirectly suggest a lover who, in the poems, is often directly addressed: 'Without you green apples wouldn't taste greener... Without you Clark Kent would forget how to become Superman'.

In 1967, alongside Roger McGough and Brian Patten, Henri staged a series of *Love Nights*, multimedia happenings which combined poetry, music, light shows, dance and live painting. Eager to experiment in different forms, he wrote and performed in *Yesterday's Girl* (1973), a semi-autobiographical Granada Television play, taped with live music in front of a studio audience. He also told love stories in epistolary novels and plays written in collaboration with other writers including Nell Dunn and Carol Ann Duffy.

Fig. 22 *Joyce Collage*, 1961, mixed media on paper, 36 × 25 cm

SIMBARI oils

Y TALBOT watercolours

ER GALLERY

Street W1

LEVISSEN

82470

R

5

Joyce

COFFE

¡GO!

WHIZ

IN COMES A BRILLIANT
NEW WAY OF ENJOYING LIF

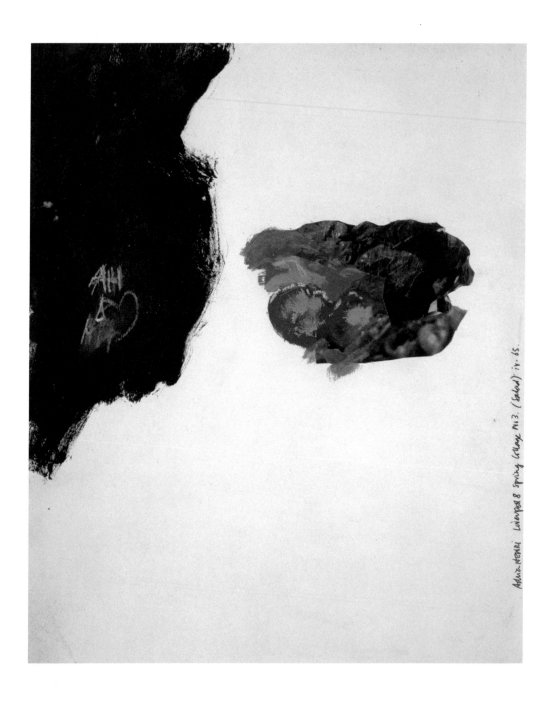

Fig. 23 *Liverpool 8 Spring Collage No. 3 (Salad)*, 1965, mixed media on paper,
32 × 26 cm

Fig. 24 *24 Collages No. 19. Summer Painting (Père Ubu with Nymphs)*, 1965,
collage and paint on paper, 54 × 45.5 cm

ICA The Institute of Contemporary Arts
Nash House The Mall London SW1

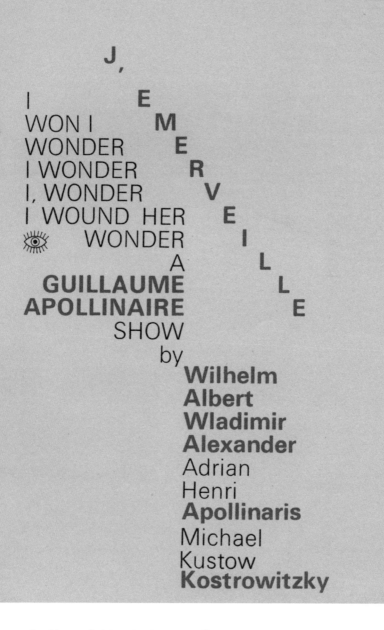

J,
I   E
WON I   M
WONDER   E
I WONDER   R
I, WONDER   V
I WOUND HER   E
WONDER   I
A   L
GUILLAUME   L
APOLLINAIRE   E
SHOW
by
Wilhelm
Albert
Wladimir
Alexander
Adrian
Henri
Apollinaris
Michael
Kustow
Kostrowitzky

Fig. 25 Programme for *J'émerveille/I Wonder* show on Guillaume Apollinaire,
ICA, London, 1968

Fig. 26 Poster for *Love Love Love: The New Poetry* (London: Corgi Books, 1967)

I LOVE YOU
YOU

on trains
in cars
on buses
in taxis
I LOVE YOU
in that midnight hour
when all the clocks stopped
and it was midsummer
forever
Have you
heard
the
Amazing Adventures of

THE LIVERPOOL SCENE?

Produced by John Peel
and featuring these amazing popgressives:—

Andy Roberts, Vocal, guitar	Mike Evans, Poet, tenor saxophone	Percy Jones, Bass
Adrian Henri, Poet	Mike Hart, Vocal, guitar	Brian Dodson, Drums

"THE AMAZING
ADVENTURES OF.."
© SF 7995

Jefferson Airplane
"Bless Its Pointed Little Head"
Their latest album
© RD 8019

Bend your mind to
Andromeda
Experience this new group's debut disc:
"Go Your Way"
c/w **"Keep Out Cos I'm Dying"** **RCA**
RCA 1854
Lyric reprinted by permission of the Copyright Owner, Chappell & Co. Ltd.

Fig. 27 Magazine advertisement for *The Amazing Adventures of The Liverpool Scene,*
RCA, 1968

Fig. 28 Poster for *Love Night No. 2* event at The Everyman Theatre, Liverpool, 20 June 1967

48

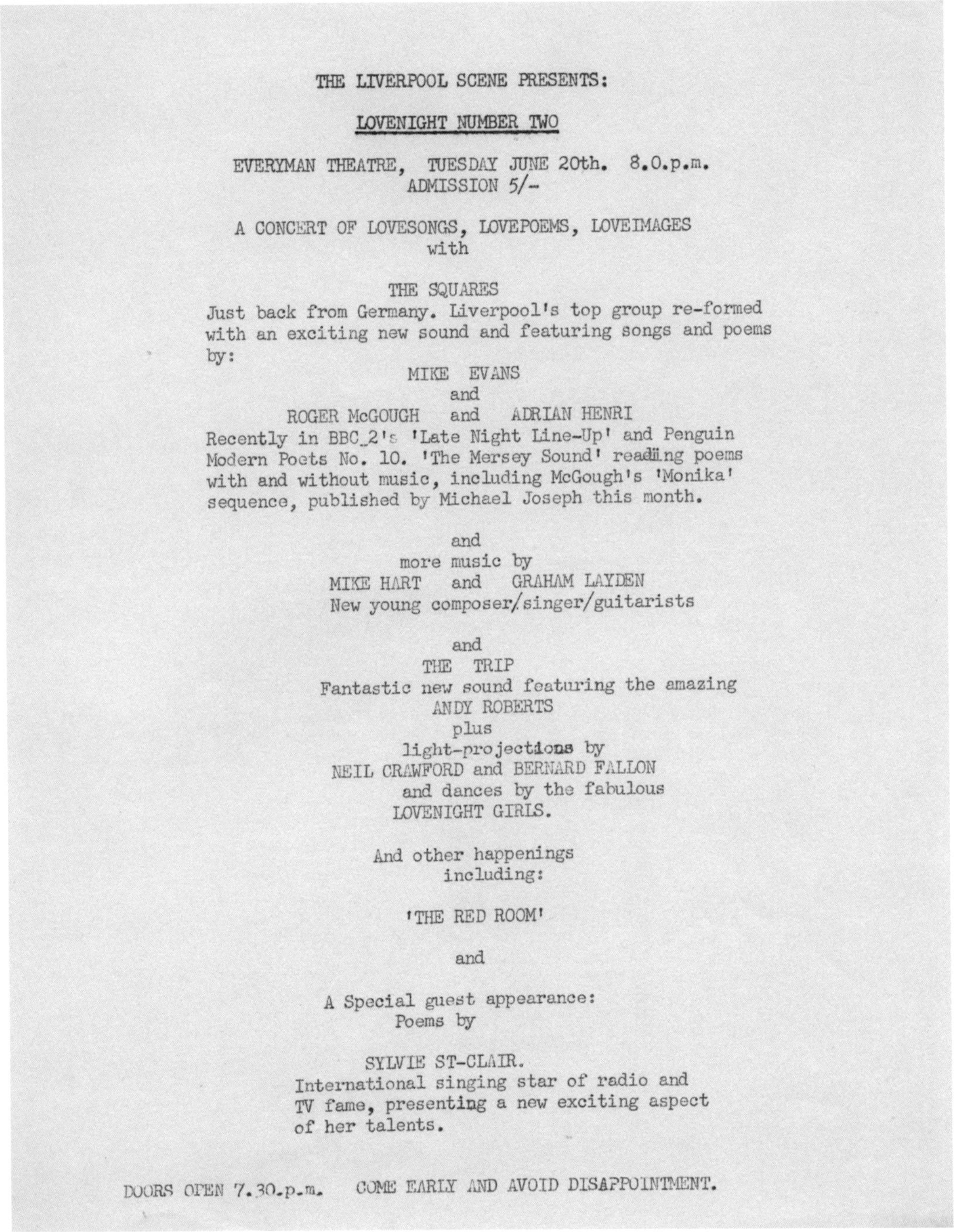

THE LIVERPOOL SCENE PRESENTS:

LOVENIGHT NUMBER TWO

EVERYMAN THEATRE, TUESDAY JUNE 20th. 8.0.p.m.
ADMISSION 5/-

A CONCERT OF LOVESONGS, LOVEPOEMS, LOVEIMAGES
with

THE SQUARES
Just back from Germany. Liverpool's top group re-formed
with an exciting new sound and featuring songs and poems
by:
MIKE EVANS
and
ROGER McGOUGH   and   ADRIAN HENRI
Recently in BBC 2's 'Late Night Line-Up' and Penguin
Modern Poets No. 10. 'The Mersey Sound' reading poems
with and without music, including McGough's 'Monika'
sequence, published by Michael Joseph this month.

and
more music by
MIKE HART   and   GRAHAM LAYDEN
New young composer/singer/guitarists

and
THE TRIP
Fantastic new sound featuring the amazing
ANDY ROBERTS
plus
light-projections by
NEIL CRAWFORD and BERNARD FALLON
and dances by the fabulous
LOVENIGHT GIRLS.

And other happenings
including:

'THE RED ROOM'

and

A Special guest appearance:
Poems by

SYLVIE ST-CLAIR.
International singing star of radio and
TV fame, presenting a new exciting aspect
of her talents.

DOORS OPEN 7.30.p.m.   COME EARLY AND AVOID DISAPPOINTMENT.

Left: **Fig. 29** *Love Night No. 2*, The Everyman Theatre, Liverpool, 20 June 1967
Leaflet and pink heart distributed to the audience during the event
Above: **Fig. 30** Script for *Love Night No. 2*

49

Which is the real ADRIAN HENRI? In Granada's Yesterday's Girl, Adrian Henri's first play for televisi (11.00), the Liverpool poet, painter, singer, writer and lover narrates a love story from his past, w three actors playing him at different ages. Left to right: Jacob Witkin, Mike Savage, the real Adri Henri and Geoffrey Evans.

Yesterday's Henri

ADRIAN HENRI, the Poet Laureate of Liverpool 8 (although his home address is in Liverpool 1) has his first play on television tonight (ITV 11.0).

It is **Yesterday's Girl**, which is really a series of dramatic flashbacks in which Henri, who gave up teaching in 1968 to become one of the father figures of the Liverpool Scene, tells the story of six years of his life and his love affair with a girl called Liz.

Says Henri, who opens the play by singing the title song: "It's a play for young people who might normally prefer to go to a pop concert. It is not a deep theatrical experience, nor is it meant to be."

He calls it "a love poem, an experiment in autobiography, a mixture of theatre and rock music—six years of my life in half an hour."

There are four Adrian Henris in this play—at age 33, Geoffrey Evans; age 36, Mike Savage; age 39, Jacob Withkin, and

TV PREVIEW by Ken Hollman

Tonight's film

8.50 (BBC-2). **THE MAN WHO CAME TO DINNER** (1941). Alexander Woolcott, said to be the original of Sheridan Whiteside, literary lion and master of the studied insult, would have approved of Monty Wooley's performance as the guest who more or less terrorises his hosts. Bette Davis (as his secretary), Ann Sheridan, Jimmy Durante.

Adrian Henri himself now.

And there is also a Liz trio—Tina Heath (at 17),

at 20 (Noreen Kershaw) and at 23 (Valerie Holliman).

Henri himself wrote the music, which is performed by the Liverpool group Sticky George.

Yesterday's Girl is from Granada, who have three major drama series going on the network—a further re-run of **A Family at War** (Monday afternoons). **Sam** (Tuesdays) and **Shabby Tiger**, the excellent adaptation of Howard Spring's first novel (Part Two, in which the artist Nick Faunt and the tempestuous Anna Fitzgerald set up house together in Manchester, is at 9.0 tonight).

BBC-1 (7.5) opens a new **Private Lives** series with the Atlantic Grey Seal, the one that lives off the British coast. Inevitably it gets involved in the right-or-wrong debate over the "culling" (killing) of 2,000 grey seals on Farne Island last year in a bid to put a check on the

seal population explo
John Webster's cla blood-and-thunder, **Duchess of Malfe**, sh previously on BBC-2. a Play of the Month run on BBC-1 (9 which gives viewers chance to see agai striking performance Eileen Atkins as tragic Duchess.

The Gates of (BBC-2, 10.25) is a six-part series in w Lord Norwich, no m narrator, explores extraordinary history the land we now call key from the civilisat of Asia Minor to coming of the Greeks

All have been fil entirely on location.

After the argum about the Channel nel (Panorama, Mond we are back again v that other fertile sou of disputation, the T London Airport, in M lin, **Right or Wro** (Man Alive, 8.0). Douglas Henry exam the case for and aga Maplin.

Left: **Fig. 31** Ken Hollman, article about *Yesterday's Girl* in the *Liverpool Daily Post*, 18 July 1973

Top: **Fig. 32** Stills from *Yesterday's Girl*, Granada Television, 1973

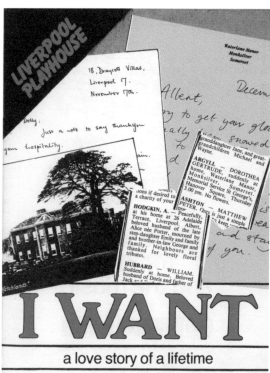

Above left: **Fig. 33** Nell Dunn and Adrian Henri, *I Want* (London: Jonathan Cape, 1972)
Above right: **Fig. 34** Programme for the premiere of *I Want*, The Liverpool Playhouse, 1983
Opposite: **Fig. 35** Poster for *Beauty and the Beast & Other Stories* by Carol Ann Duffy and
Adrian Henri, Richard Demarco Gallery, Edinburgh, 4–11 September 1978

BEAUTY and the BEAST

& other stories

NEW POEMS BY

ADRIAN HENRI   CAROL ANN DUFFY

5.15 NIGHTLY
SEPTEMBER 4th - 11th 1978

The Richard Demarco Gallery

MONTEITH HOUSE
61 HIGH STREET
EDINBURGH

Telephone
031-557 0707

Heroes

In Henri's work, homage often takes the form of allusion, parody, variation, direct or indirect quotation. His poems and paintings are a kind of 'self-portrait with badges' peopled with friends and heroes, whether real or imaginary, highbrow or popular. We find Batman cheek by jowl with Liverpool Football Club legends, André Breton with Pete Brown, Henri Rousseau with Eduardo Paolozzi, Claude Debussy with George Melly.

Henri was fascinated by figures of absurdity too, in particular King Ubu, the preposterous autocrat created by Alfred Jarry. He wrote an adaptation of Jarry's play, relocated to Liverpool, and played the part of Ubu, whom he considered as a gloriously pathetic alter ego. Giving full rein to his taste for anarchy and for a 'systematic derangement of the senses', he also collaborated with performance artist Robert Conybear, known as Rob Con, who orchestrated Henri's mock multi-media funeral.

Opposite: **Fig. 36** *24 Collages No. 4, Clayton Squares Painting* (detail), 1964, collage and paint on paper, 54 × 45.5 cm
Following spread: **Fig. 37** *The Entry of Christ into Liverpool in 1964*, 1962–64, oil on hessian, 183 × 243.8 cm

THE ENTRY OF CHRIST INTO LIV
HOMAGE TO JA

SOCIALISM

GUINNESS

COOPER

POOL IN 1964 ADRIAN HENRI
ES ENSOR 1962-64

Now the procession

THE MARCHING DRUMS
hideous masked Breughel faces of old ladies in the crowd
yellow masks of girls in curlers and headscarves
smelling of factories

MASKS   MASKS   MASKS

red masks   purple masks   pink masks
crushing surging carrying me along
down the hill past the Philharmonic The Labour Exchange
excited feet crushing the geraniums in St. Luke's Gardens
placards   banners   posters

KEEP BRITTAIN WHITE
END THE WAR IN VIETNAM
GOD BLESS OUR POPE

Billboards hoardings drawings on pavements

words painted on the road
STOP   GO   HALT
the sounds of pipes and drums down the street
little girls in yellow and orange dresses paper flowers
embroidered banners

LOYAL SONS OF KING WILLIAM LODGE BOOTLE

MASKS more MASKS crowding in off buses
standing on walls climbing fences
familiar faces among the crowd
faces of my friends   the shades of Pierre Bonnard   and
Guillaume Apollinaire
Jarry cycling carefully through the crowd.
A black cat picking her way underfoot
posters
signs
gleaming salads
Colmans Mustard
J. Ensor, Fabriqueur de Masques
HAIL JESUS, KING OF THE JEWS
straining forward to catch a glimpse through the crowd

red hair   white robe   grey donkey
familiar face
traffic lights   zebra crossings
GUIN
GUINN
GUINNESS IS
white bird dying unnoticed in a corner
splattered feathers
blood running merged with the neon signs
in a puddle

Opposite: **Fig. 38** *The Entry of Christ into Liverpool*, poster-poem (detail), published
by the ICA, London, 1968, 126 × 30 cm

Above: **Fig. 39** *24 Collages No. 10 (Homage to Paolozzi)*, 1966, mixed media on paper, 54 × 46cm

Following spread: **Fig. 40** *Batcomposition*, 1967, collage on card, 52 × 78 cm

B

The rota blades are shattered and Rob[...]
Batman bail out from the crippled batc[...]
it crashes. Their escape is witnessed by[...]
little man.

POW!

BUMPER
SOUVENIR
CATALOGUE

JULES FEIFFER!
DENIS GIFFORD!
ADRIAN HENRI!"
STAN LEE!
GEO. MELLY!
ADRIAN MITCHELL!
GEO. ORWELL!
GEO. PERRY!
ROBERT WARSHOW!

AAARGH!

A CELEBRATION OF **COMICS** AT THE INSTITUTE OF (GULP!?*) **CONTEMPORARY ARTS** IN THE MALL

Opposite: **Fig. 41** *AAARGH! A Celebration of Comics*,
exhibition catalogue, ICA, London, 1970
Above: **Fig. 42** *Bronco* event at The Blue Angel nightclub,
Liverpool, c. 1968 (with Allan Williams)
Left: **Fig. 43** Adrian Henri's Batmask

Above: **Fig. 44** Adrian Henri's badge collection
Opposite: **Fig. 45** *Kop II* (detail), 1977, acrylic on canvas, 50.8 × 61 cm

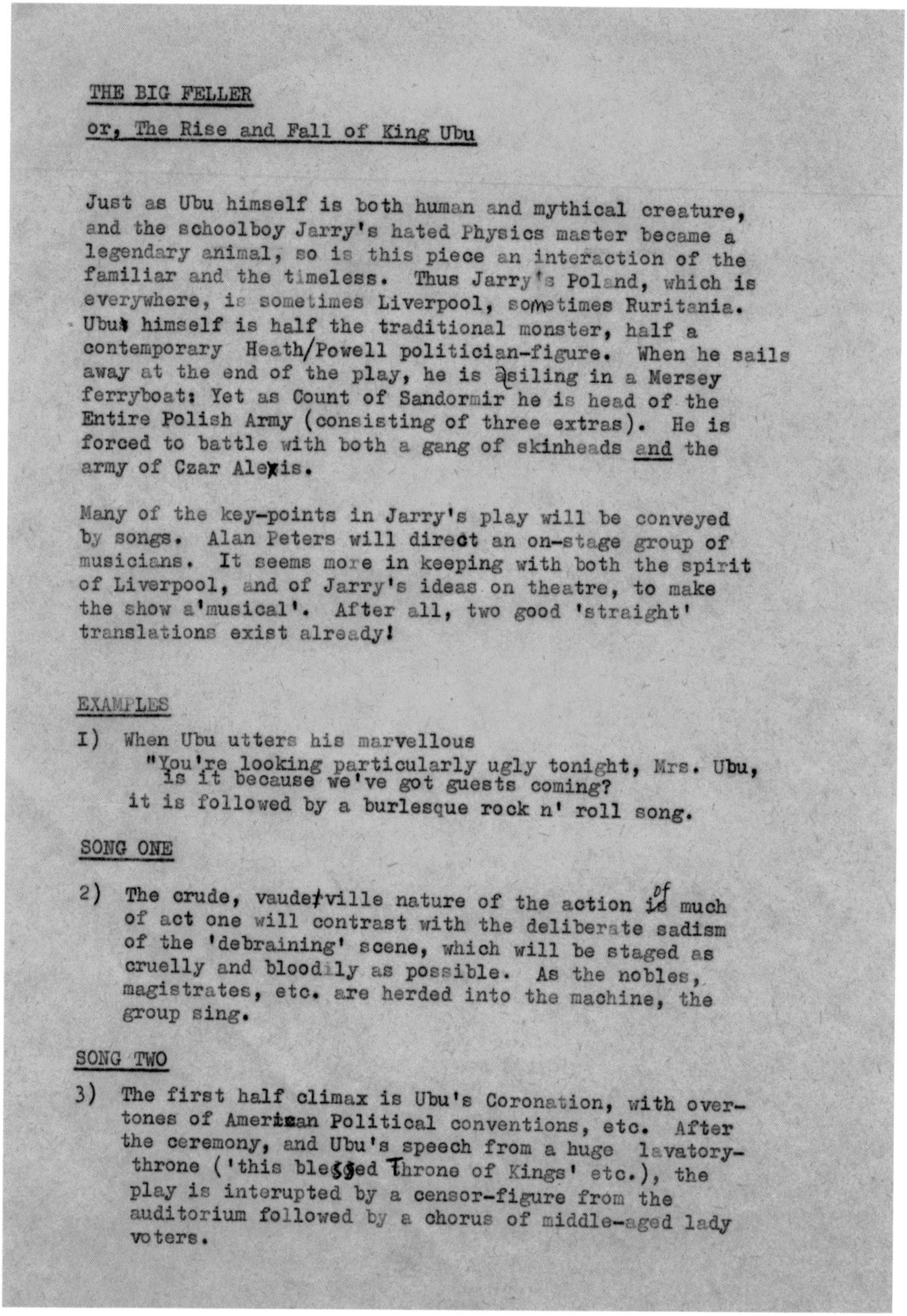

THE BIG FELLER

or, The Rise and Fall of King Ubu

Just as Ubu himself is both human and mythical creature,
and the schoolboy Jarry's hated Physics master became a
legendary animal, so is this piece an interaction of the
familiar and the timeless. Thus Jarry's Poland, which is
everywhere, is sometimes Liverpool, sometimes Ruritania.
Ubu himself is half the traditional monster, half a
contemporary Heath/Powell politician-figure. When he sails
away at the end of the play, he is sailing in a Mersey
ferryboat: Yet as Count of Sandormir he is head of the
Entire Polish Army (consisting of three extras). He is
forced to battle with both a gang of skinheads and the
army of Czar Alexis.

Many of the key-points in Jarry's play will be conveyed
by songs. Alan Peters will direct an on-stage group of
musicians. It seems more in keeping with both the spirit
of Liverpool, and of Jarry's ideas on theatre, to make
the show a 'musical'. After all, two good 'straight'
translations exist already!

EXAMPLES

I) When Ubu utters his marvellous
       "You're looking particularly ugly tonight, Mrs. Ubu,
        is it because we've got guests coming?
    it is followed by a burlesque rock n' roll song.

SONG ONE

2) The crude, vaudeville nature of the action is much
    of act one will contrast with the deliberate sadism
    of the 'debraining' scene, which will be staged as
    cruelly and bloodily as possible. As the nobles,
    magistrates, etc. are herded into the machine, the
    group sing.

SONG TWO

3) The first half climax is Ubu's Coronation, with over-
    tones of American Political conventions, etc. After
    the ceremony, and Ubu's speech from a huge lavatory-
    throne ('this blessed Throne of Kings' etc.), the
    play is interupted by a censor-figure from the
    auditorium followed by a chorus of middle-aged lady
    voters.

Fig. 46 *The Big Feller, or, The Rise and Fall of King Ubu*, Adrian Henri's
adaptation of Alfred Jarry's play, c. 1966

Fig. 47 The Liverpool Scene, poster, late 1960s

Above: **Fig. 48** Adrian Henri as King Ubu, Bradford, 1975
Right: **Fig. 49** Ubu sculpture and plate, presented to Adrian Henri by
students from Bradford Art College, where he was visiting lecturer, 1975
(photographed on the staircase of his house in Liverpool)

""Sanity as a Complete Fallacy""

Adrian/Rob Con.人 3/5/'75.

Above: **Fig. 50** Rob Con and Adrian Henri, *Sanity as a Complete Fallacy*, performance, 1975
Opposite, from top to bottom: **Fig. 51** Card from Rob Con to Adrian Henri, 1974; **Fig. 52**
Card from Adrian Henri to Rob Con, 1971; **Fig. 53** Card from Rob Con to Adrian Henri, 1978

"Behold I stand at your door and write,
A Poem to be posted at midnight."

(Adrian Henri and Vincent Price)

Rob Con:/—
20/1/74.

---

21 Mount St, Liverpool I

dear Rob
        One of the bits of your foam party-suit
fell from my pocket onto the pavement between
I9 and 2I Mount St Liverpool at approximately
I7.58 on Tues. 29th June I97I.
                                        Adrian

Adrian, Could you please let me
have a list of things you like,
have affinity or obsession with..
as an aid to my designing for the
'Funeral' catagories broader the
better. If to° buisy we'll do one
the next time I see you aparently
in a few weeks time...

Yours Best of Imagination.

Rob Conybeare.

Black-Embryo-shaped Dart-board for Poems in Flight..

Rob Con:/k
14/1/76.

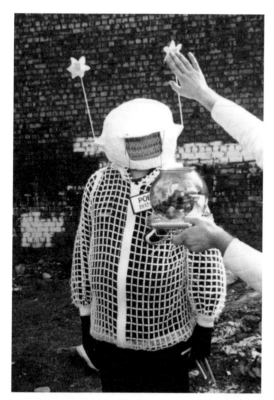

Opposite: **Fig. 54** *Funeral of Adrian Henri*, performance by Rob Con and
Adrian Henri, with Lol Coxhill, Roger McGough and others, Liverpool, 28 April 1979
Above, top: **Fig. 55** Invitation to the *Funeral of Adrian Henri*, 1979
Above, bottom: **Fig. 56** Rob Con, sculpted map of the funeral procession, 1979,
31 × 25 × 10 cm

America!

In the early 1960s, having not long emerged from the austerity of the postwar years, many British artists looked to the US rather than Europe for inspiration. Henri had strong affinities with the Beat poets and Pop painters who challenged established canons and traditions, and he relished the freedom of jazz musicians who experimented with new forms and structures. Yet this admiration for America's freedoms was not wholesale: he adopted a critical stance against right-wing Republican politicians in his 1964 *Anti-Goldwater Painting* dedicated to the jazz-blues singer Jimmy Witherspoon, or against the Vietnam War in his *Batpoem*.

Collage was used as a scrapbook and visual diary, as in the 1969 *New York* series, made from material collected during a tour of America with The Liverpool Scene. Through collage, whatever the iconography, Henri explored the tensions between abstract and figurative, gestural and hard-edge, hand-painted and mechanically reproduced. In poems and pictures, he thus transformed 'heaps of broken images' into dynamic and balanced compositions.

Fig. 57 *Kennedy Painting*, 25 November 1963, mixed media on paper, 36 × 28 cm

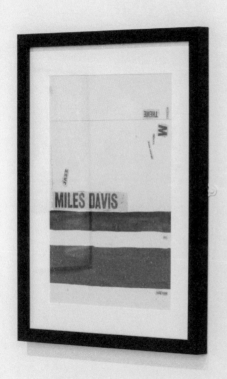

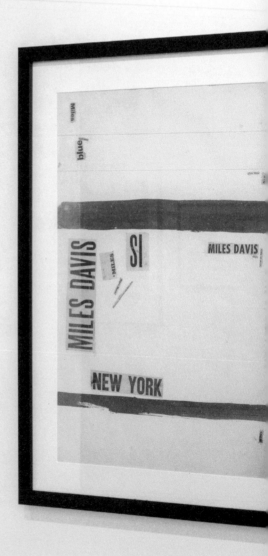

From left to right: **Fig. 58** *Homage to Miles Davis II (Blue in Green)*, 2 October 1960, mixed media on paper, 38 × 30 cm; **Fig. 59** *Homage to Miles Davis I (Kind of Blue)*, 2 October 1960, mixed media on paper, 55 × 38 cm; **Fig. 60** *Homage to Miles Davis III (Miles Ahead)*, 2 October 1960, mixed media on paper, 50 × 32 cm

Fig. 61 *24 Collages No. 1. Anti-Goldwater Painting for Jimmy Witherspoon*, 1964,
mixed media on paper, 53.5 × 45 cm

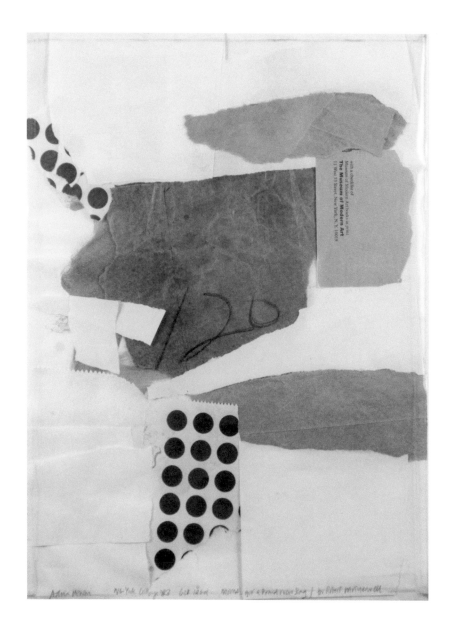

Fig. 62 *New York Collage No. 3, Homage to Robert Motherwell*, 1969,
mixed media on paper, 41 × 29.5 cm

Fig. 63 *New York Collage No. 6, Self-Portrait for Susan (with Hero)*, 1969
mixed media on paper, 41 × 29.5 cm

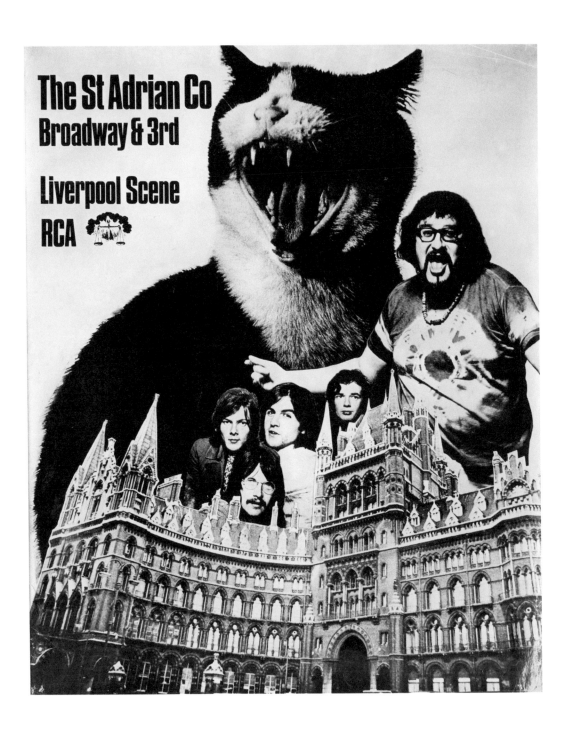

Fig. 64 Poster for The Liverpool Scene album *St Adrian Co. Broadway & 3rd*, RCA, 1970

Fig. 65 Adrian Henri and Allen Ginsberg in Holland Park, London, 1967

Fig. 66 Allen Ginsberg, *Howl and Other Poems* (San Francisco: City Lights Books, 1956) inscribed and signed by Ginsberg, who stayed with Henri during his visit to Liverpool in May 1965

Top: **Fig. 67** Adrian Henri and Ted Joans,
New York, 1969, contact sheet
Right: **Fig. 68** Poster for *Chocolate Astonishment*,
a happening by Ted Joans, with Adrian Henri,
Mike Evans and others, Traverse Theatre,
Edinburgh, 1967

Traverse Poets
Workshop
present

ChocolateAstonishment
by
ted Joans
today Sunday Sept. 3
3:PM-6:PM
in the bar room
A Happening! Now!

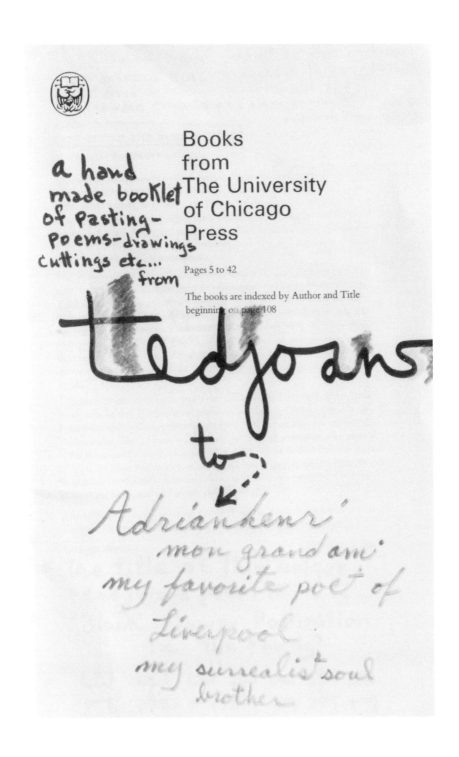

Fig. 69 Ted Joans, *a hand-made booklet of pasting – poems – drawings – cuttings etc...*, 1969

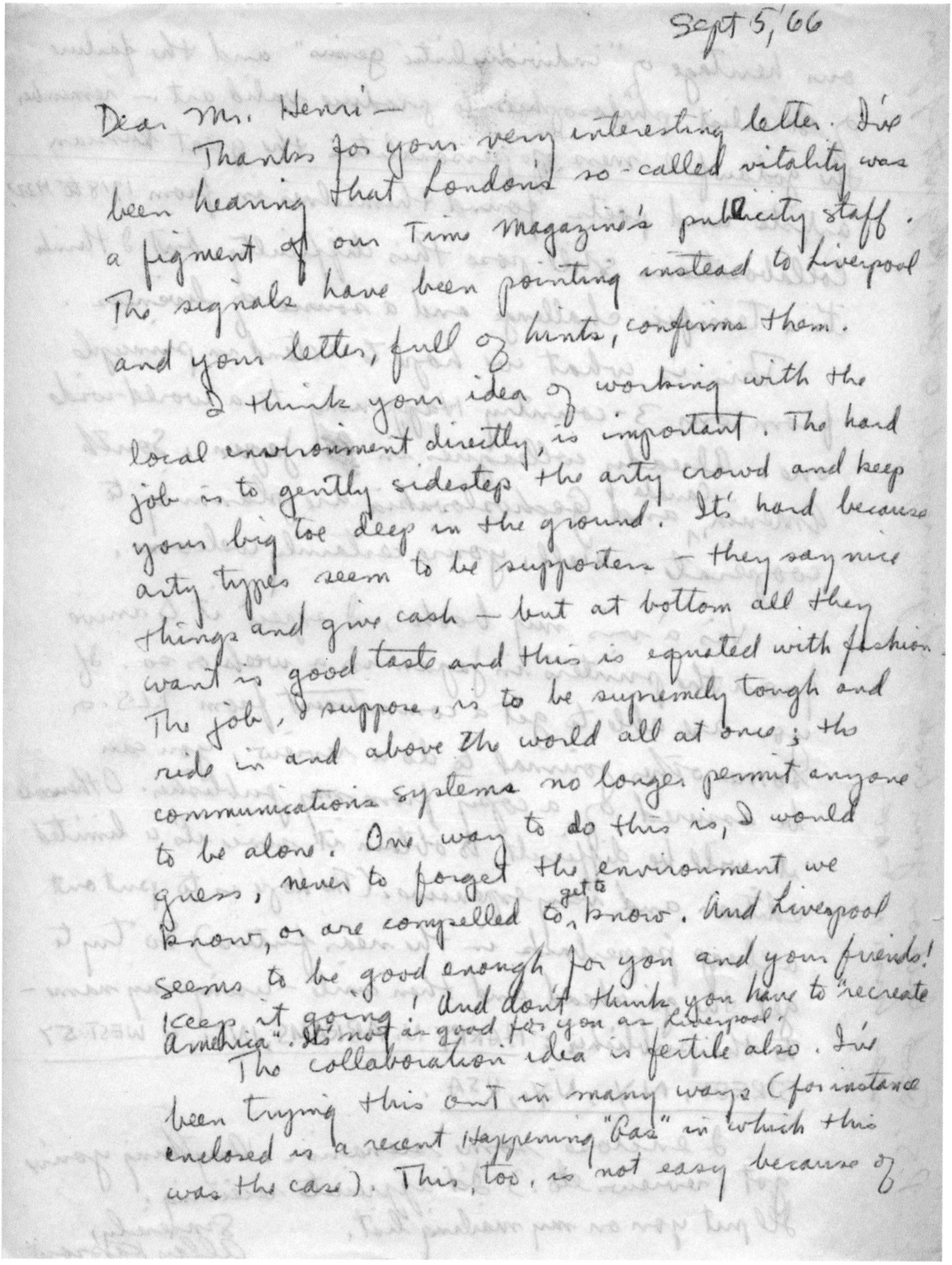

Sept 5, '66

Dear Mr. Henri —

Thanks for your very interesting letter. I've been hearing that London's so-called vitality was a figment of our Time Magazine's publicity staff. The signals have been pointing instead to Liverpool and your letter, full of hints, confirms them.

I think your idea of working with the local environment directly, is important. The hard job is to gently sidestep the arty crowd and keep your big toe deep in the ground! It's hard because arty types seem to be supporters — they say nice things and give cash — but at bottom all they want is good taste and this is equated with fashion. The job, I suppose, is to be supremely tough and ride in and above the world all at once; the communications systems no longer permit anyone to be alone! One way to do this is, I would guess, never to forget the environment we know, or are compelled to get to know. And Liverpool seems to be good enough for you and your friends! Keep it going! And don't think you have to "recreate America". It's not as good for you as Liverpool.

The collaboration idea is fertile also. I've been trying this out in many ways (for instance enclosed is a recent Happening "Gas" in which this was the case). This, too, is not easy because of

Fig. 70 Letter from Allan Kaprow to Adrian Henri, 5 September 1966

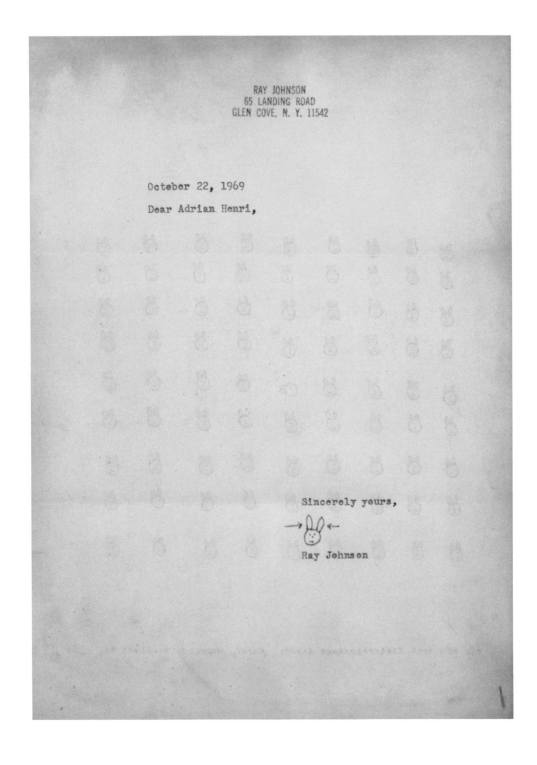

Fig. 71 Letter from Ray Johnson to Adrian Henri, 1969

Fig. 72 George Brecht with Ray Johnson, New York Correspondence School
Meeting leaflet, undated (c.1969)

yoko ono

MUSIC OF THE MIND & TUES SEPT 26 7:30PM
'THE FOG MACHINE'

THE BLUECOAT SOCIETY OF ARTS
BLUECOAT CHAMBERS SCHOOL LA

TICKETS 5' & 7'6 at CRANES HANOVER ST & LIVERPOOL COLLEGE OF ART

Top: **Fig. 73** Adrian Henri wrapping Yoko Ono for her *Fog Piece*, the Bluecoat,
Liverpool, 26 September 1967
Bottom: **Fig. 74** Poster for *Fog Piece* at the Bluecoat, Liverpool

Bread on the Night

From 1961, alongside Roger McGough and Brian Patten, Henri was instrumental in establishing Liverpool's poetry scene. They organised live readings at a variety of venues – the upstairs room of a bar, the basement of a theatre, occasionally The Cavern club – and attracted a young audience who, as McGough recalls, 'didn't look on it as Poetry with a capital P, they looked on it as modern entertainment, part of the pop movement'.

There was no shortage of bands in the city, and musicians often took part in those readings, either backing poets or singing between their sets. Some of those collaborations led to the formation of groups like The Scaffold whose 'Lily the Pink' reached number one in the UK pop charts, or The Liverpool Scene, with their experimental mixture of poetry, politics, vaudeville and rock and roll.

Fig. 75 Fans of The Liverpool Scene, Molde International Jazz Festival, Norway, 1970

ALL ABOUT 'THE LIVERPOOL SCENE'

A new concept in pop music/ entertainment

STATEMENT

In the last ten years there have been two new tendencies in the arts: towards
a fusion of the various art forms, and towards an awareness of the need to
entertain. The young American artist Andy Warhol, for instance, is well known
as a film-maker and also as manager of a new beat group, 'The Velvet Underground'. Two examples of the new 'intermedia' activities are Happenings and
Jazz-and-poetry.

In 1962 Roger McGough and I presented 'City', the first Liverpool 'event',
(Happening). These mixed-media theatre-pieces moved towards a new involv-
ment with the audience, and later included local groups, like 'The Roadrunners' (led by Mike Hart) and the Clayton Squares, (in which Mike Evans
played saxophone and sang.)

Both McGough and I had tried reading to jazz accompaniment and found this
unsatisfactory. We came to feel that 'beat' music, which is basically
meant to accompany words, and is seldom purely instrumental, was a more
suitable field for collaboration. Later Andy Roberts, with a growing
reputation in the folk world, began working out more complex arrangements to
fit the poems. Some of these are to be heard on CBS LP 63045, (The Incredible
New Liverpool Scene). In folk music too, the music should complement the
words.

Recently, in the work of Lennon-McCartney, Bob Dylan, Christopher Logue,
Paul Simon, Adrian Mitchell, Sydney Carter, Donovan and groups like the
Incredible String Band and the Mothers of Invention, the worlds of pop, folk
and poetry have come to an area of agreement about the relationship of words
and music.

Our aim is to have a semi-permanent musical/literary roadshow, which
would include the five group members for engagements and the group
augmented with extra musicians, light projectionist, dancers, etc. for
bigger shows, concerts or dances. We prefer to be looked on as a group
rather than individuals. We all live in the same house and share the
same common assumptions: we are hoping for greater possibilities for
collaboration within the group, and to reach a new and ever growing
audience.

Adrian Henri.

Fig. 76 Adrian Henri, The Liverpool Scene statement, c. 1968

Fig. 77 Poster for The Liverpool Scene, *The Amazing Adventures of...*, RCA, 1968

Fig. 78 UFO Coming: The Crazy World of Arthur Brown/The Soft Machine,
16 June 1967 & The Liverpool Love Festival, 23 June 1967, UFO Club, London
(poster design by Hapshash and the Coloured Coat)

my people were fair
and had sky in their hair......
but now they're content
to wear stars on their brows

TYRANNOSAURUS REX

    Marc Bolan .... vocals, guitar
    Steve Peregrine Took .. vocals, bongos

LIVERPOOL SCENE

    Adrian Henri .... lead poet
    Andy Roberts .... lead ans acoustic guitar
    Mike Evans .... poet and saxophonist
    Mike Hart .... vocals and rhythm guitar
    Percy Jones .... bass
    Brian Dobson .... drums

JOHN PEEL .... words

Fig. 79 Programme for In The Sticks, with Tyrannosaurus Rex, The Liverpool
Scene and John Peel at City Memorial Hall, Sheffield, 17 June 1968

Fig. 80 The Liverpool Scene, albums, publicity material and press cuttings, 1968–72

Above: **Fig. 81** Poster for The Liverpool Scene, Warwick University Jazz Club,
3 May 1969
Opposite: **Fig. 82** Poster for The Liverpool Scene, Mothers (formerly Carlton
Ballroom), Erdington, Birmingham, 23 May 1969
Following spread: **Fig. 83** Promotional photo, The Liverpool Scene, c. 1969

MOTHERS

FRI. 23 MAY
LIVERPOOL
SCENE

ERDINGTON

Fig. 84 From left to right: The Liverpool Scene promotional folder; photo of Robert Plant and Jimmy Page wearing the Bobby and the Helmets t-shirt (Newport Jazz Festival, 1969); back cover of *Bread on the Night* (RCA 1969), with Henri wearing the Bobby t-shirt, Bobby's helmet, kaleidoscopic glasses and badge; *The Woo-Woo* single (RCA, 1969)

Fig. 85 Poster for The Liverpool Scene, Warwick University, 10 January 1970

Fig. 86 Poster for The Liverpool Scene, University College London, 1969

Fig. 87 Poster for Pop Proms, Royal Albert Hall, London, 1969
(The Liverpool Scene supported Led Zeppelin on 29 June)

Fig. 88 Poster for The Liverpool Scene May Day concert at the Student Union, Edgbaston, Birmingham, 1974

Notes
on Painting
and Poetry

Adrian Henri (1968)

1. *On being a painter and poet*
The trouble is that people want a label for you. I find in practice no difficulty (other than shortage of time) in doing two things full time, not to mention teaching, doing readings, organising or helping with theatre pieces. Kurt Schwitters solved the problem beautifully by having a catchall name for his activities: 'MERZ'. Typically and beautifully meaningless, MERZ specifies a whole spectrum of activities: MERZpoem, MERZtheatre, MERZpainting, MERZhouse, MERZcolumn. Other painter/poets or poet/painters have had the advantage of a movement which gave them a label: Arp, Breton, Tzara, Cocteau, Ernst. In both Dada and Surrealism perhaps the most significant concept was that of the total work – '*Gesamtkunstwerk*' – or that of the total man. Consider Duchamp, or the prewar activities of Salvador Dalí: films, exhibition-environments, poems, book jackets, objects, ephemeral events are equally important in their oeuvre. And there are dozens of young artists whom it is almost impossible to label – Dick Higgins, George Brecht, Red Grooms, Robert Whitman, Daniel Spoerri, Robert Morris, Jackson MacLow, Allan Kaprow, La Monte Young. These 'intermedia' artists, and pop artists generally, are of course working in a direct line of descent from the Dada/Surrealist tradition.

2. When one considers the problems involved in learning to be a poet it's amazing just how many good ones actually survive. Consider the difference between a would-be poet and a would-be painter. The poet has no possibility of going to poetry school to learn. Perhaps as well! Instead he learns by familiarising himself with the work of other poets living and dead. By finding out about their working procedures and assumptions. And by reading the pronouncements of theorists. It is at this point that the poet writing in English runs up against a brick wall whichever direction he goes. For here he encounters the insularity, exclusivity and chauvinism of so many critics, professors and theorists. In an article in the *Times Literary Supplement* recently, A. Alvarez spent some four closely reasoned pages summarising the modern tradition in literature and coming to the conclusion that only four recent poets have produced work of any value: of these one had committed suicide, the others were mentally unstable and one produced uneven work anyway. And their subject matter was always their own isolation, their own neurosis. What a miserable and hopeless view of the possibilities of literature, and of the whole cultural tradition of the twentieth century! What a denial of joy, of the most amazing creative outburst since the Renaissance. Furthermore, what is appalling is that the average young writer aspires to do Eng. Lit., if possible at Oxbridge. There he is handed a similarly restrictive set of rules and assumptions along with his ready-torn brand new undergrad gown the first day he gets there. And most of them never really look any further. Poetry reviewing in England is done by a tiny handful of people who as educated men must be aware of other literatures but whose view of English literature seems completely untouched by this. Even bad art critics, on the other hand, have to relate specific painters to general movements in international terms.

The most coherent short conspectus of the modern movement in literature I know is contained in a chapter in Moholy-Nagy's *Vision in Motion*. This is in fact an art teacher's sourcebook describing his design course at MIT. I wouldn't think most students of literature would be likely to come across it: art students would.

Now consider the would-be painter. If he goes to the worst art college in England and ends up as a very bad painter indeed he must have one tremendous advantage: that even the worst painter when he exhibits a painting now relates himself to the whole twentieth-century tradition in the arts whether he wants to or not, his work implicitly states where he stands in relation to it. Because even the worst art school teaches not just the cuisine of art, how to draw and mix colour and so on, but an implied attitude to one's work and one's self that can best be summarised by quoting Robert Motherwell:

> I believe that painters' judgements of painting are first ethical, then aesthetic, the aesthetic judgements flowing from ethical contexts (Statement for *The New American Painting*, 1957).

Elsewhere he says that when one painter says to another 'He is a good painter' he is making an ethical statement not an aesthetic one, he means his attitude to his work is admirable rather than that he makes beautiful pictures. This is why we revere painters like Cézanne and Jackson Pollock who were by no means 'good' in a purely academic sense. In passing we might wonder just how many practicing poets, whose business is words, write as consistently intelligently and incisively on the theory of the craft as Motherwell. Even the averagely good painter has some kind of personal aesthetic which, as I said above, shows where he stands vis-à-vis society and the work of others. And the faculty of self-criticism that doesn't allow him to repeat earlier achievements but strive towards a new and fresh form for which he has to say. The good experimental artist tries to see just how much a technique, a tradition can stand before it reaches breaking point.

3. An obvious reply to 2 would be a variation on the old 'If-you-don't-like-England-why-do-you-stay-here?' argument beloved of alehouse political commentators. Why do I write poems? Because I believe poetry is bigger than all the restrictions I've mentioned. The Liverpool painter Robin Rae said to me that what was rather chastening about going abroad was how much Italians can tell you about Italian writers, which makes you realise how little you really know about your own. And that nevertheless English poetry has the finest and fullest unbroken tradition of any modern language. England hasn't any such continuous tradition in the visual arts. And poetry is a more natural, instinctive form of expression than any other, I think. *'Il chante comme l'homme respire'* seems to me a marvellous thing for someone to say of you.

One amazing thing about becoming known as a poet is the number of people who give you poems to look at in pubs, on buses, by letter, in the street. Total strangers or people you have known for years. Perhaps most of them bad, but how good is it that housewives, bus conductors, sociology students and schoolgirls want to express something and poetry is the most natural means to say it. Because the only *physical* technique required is the ability to write or speak English and the only equipment a pencil and a piece of paper. Or a tape recorder. What amateur poets don't realise of course is the techniques are just as hard to master as in other art forms but basically non-physical. To express anything in a given art form seems to me to need an amount of technique and equipment in ascending order as listed: poetry, painting, sculpture, music. As I have said elsewhere (*The Liverpool Scene*, 71) the reason I write poetry and give readings is that done that way it is a more complete communications-mechanism. I am aware of the audience reaction as a painter can never be. I think this urge to communicate is also one of the major factors in the development of happenings with US painters around 1960.

4. As a poet I am interested in how far poetry can be pushed in different directions and still remain poetry. (This is, as I have suggested above, very much a painter's ethic.) Can a poem be a letter? A news item? A cut-up of disparate material? A concrete typographic statement that couldn't be read out? At one time I tried writing 'poems without words' simple action-pieces or instructions for the audience to see if it was possible to create a poetic image without verbalising at all. When Brian Patten and I wrote 'Night' we called it a 'Poem with and without words': an alternating sequence of verbal or visual images. Tzara offered a very different account of how to make a poem from the one accepted in 1916:

To make a dadaist poem
Take a newspaper
Take a pair of scissors...
(*Dada Manifesto* No. VIII)

I have always thought the best one-word definition of art is 'metamorphosis'. Picasso's life is a constant day-to-day demonstration of this. When Shelley wanted to send a present to a girl he chose to write the note that went with it in verse. 'With a guitar, to Jane' is still a living poem which anyone can read and enjoy. A note in prose would probably have been thrown away and if not would at best provide perhaps a footnote to the biographer. What makes the poetry is, of course, the crucial factor, X, The Magic Ingredient, and involves almost purely formal factors. If the words don't combine properly it still isn't poetry. In the same way that a painter can have a marvellous idea for a painting but what we see is the result of the interaction between this idea and what happens in a physical application of the paint to canvas. How can we judge? I think the only way a poet can tell is by using the whole of his experience of literature to develop the faculty of judging whether this work remains poetry or not. This is the value of tradition, real tradition, the living tradition of the language and literature of a people, *not* a set of rules that were invented because they seemed to be expedient to a given person at a given time, and which remain to litter the groves of Academe.

D.H. Lawrence seems to me one of the most important poets in English because his mature work demonstrates how someone can develop a completely new and personal set of formal procedures apt for what he is saying at the time and developed through awareness of this process in other, earlier writers. This is much more important than all that fuss about sex and Dark Gods. The other factor for me is that of audience-communication. This worries a lot more traditionally 'literary' people – they feel that if the poem can be got across at one hearing then it *can't* be any good. This is to ignore the fact that until the coming of cheap printed books and universal literacy this was the only way that most people could experience the theatre or even most poetry. And similarly with music before cheap recordings were available. The new art forms like jazz and the cinema function almost entirely in this way. To say that this means you can't subject a Charlie Parker solo or a sequence from *Potemkin* to close analysis is plainly ludicrous. It is just that it is not often possible for non-specialists to do so. Eliot once said: 'Genuine poetry can communicate before it is understood' and is certainly true of him. And of Joyce. What carries you along in both cases is the *music*: as the Duchess might have said 'Take care of the sounds, and the sense will take care of itself'. What is important about Eliot's much-quoted dictum is that it differentiates between 'communication' and 'understanding'. This is patently true in music: no one would suggest that you can't enjoy Beethoven the first time you hear it. Equally no one would suggest that you would get everything from it at one go. What I *aim* at doing (whether this ever happens is another matter) is writing something that *does* communicate when you hear it, but which has other layers of meaning that can be understood by reading it on the printed page, at home. What may well prove the final death-blow to Poetry with a capital P is that in some spheres communication has become an exact science. The average poem in, say, *The Review* would fare badly if subjected to the Occam's Razor of the communications engineer. 'Information is that which removes uncertainty': the more uncertainty removed the higher its value. Anything else is irrelevant.

5. *A note on improvisation*
Improvisation seems to me to be a greatly overrated factor in recent art. Except in that any artwork could be said to be improvisational in origin: there isn't much work done entirely to order these days, except perhaps film music. Some of the English poetry-and-jazz people make exaggerated claims about this and some poets I know are constantly re-writing their work. It seems to me axiomatic that if a thing is worth saying it is worth saying properly. In other words there is one

way and one way only of saying what you want to say in the most precise and clear way possible. It may take much writing and re-writing to find it, of course. For the reasons stated above I believe that the 'formal' or perhaps better 'musical' values are what makes poetry poetry. And anyway real improvisation is pretty rare. One great misconception about happenings, for example, is that they are improvised, or just 'happen'. Nothing could be further from the truth. Kaprow often used a strict timing sequence or a code of movement notation like that of Laban. Oldenburg used a system of lights in 'Fotodeath' to regulate the action. I use music as a limiting factor in mine. It determines the length and sequence of the piece. Almost all are strictly scripted. What does happen is that the performer can make small existential alterations to details in performance: the crowd may fill a space free at rehearsal, for instance. The apparently random works of John Cage and his followers are in fact called 'aleatory' rather than 'improvised'. Cage's music is exactly programmed as Bach, what is left is freedom for the performer to alter the predetermined sequence if necessary. Even jazz improvisation is usually 'on the chords of' a fixed sequence. The new-wave jazz that often sounds formless is in fact often based on an extra-musical limitation of a given mood or colour as in Indian music.

What is basically exciting about jazz or the cinema is that 'communication' and 'understanding' occur at best almost simultaneously. In jazz this is true of the performer as well. Painters like Pollock and Mathieu rely on their developed instincts and skills when 'improvising' a painting. I think a good war photographer like Robert Capa or Don McCullin is a perfect example of this – you see an incident about to happen and all the purely technical decisions about focus, exposure, etc., are made in the time it takes to raise the camera and press the shutter. I think it was Julius Caesar who first said that style consisted of learning all the rules and then forgetting them. Having said this I must now say that I do occasionally improvise in performance. Usually it is the same one or two poems which I add to or subtract from. Particularly 'I Want to Paint' because its episodic construction allows addition of extra lines according to circumstances. The best of the added bits have in fact stayed in – the original poem was written in 1961 and was in fact about half its present length. The only copy of this was eventually lost. It was rewritten from memory and expanded for a 1964 issue of *Solem* (Manchester University) about Communications. It was again re-written in January 1966 for an issue of *Flourish* (Royal Shakespeare Company magazine) and some weak lines left out and the best of the improvised ones added.[1] Also when I started doing readings I used to find sometimes that I'd written bits in older, i.e. pre-reading, poems that I couldn't say. Obviously these were altered in reading. The interesting thing is that in every case this improved the purely literary value of the line of phrase – it was simpler, clearer, more direct. I'm never *conscious* of doing it, but I suppose now one writes with the underlying assumption 'If you can't say it, don't write it'. As a general rule this would be tough on poets with speech defects I suppose. I have a fantasy about writing a poem that one poet of my acquaintance just couldn't read.

6. If poetry read aloud is a good communications system, then painting is a bad one: you make it in isolation and it goes to a gallery or to someone's house and you never really know how people react to it. I don't think this is necessarily a bad thing. I do think it's necessary to be aware of the difference. When I only wrote poetry as a sort of sideline, my pictures were often quite literary in content – I am thinking of pictures from the early 1960s like *Interior, The Simultaneous and Historical Faces of Death* and the *Piccadilly Manchester* series. Since I have written more regularly I find I paint perhaps slightly less but when I do I think the images work in more purely visual terms. The *Death of a Bird in the City* series has always been a fairly 'pure' sort of visual image to me. The recent paintings of salads, meat or cakes are 'pure' in a different way: the image is presented extra-clear, extra-bright, in isolation. Not particularly placed anywhere in the canvas to make it interesting compositionally. And in a sort of spatial limbo. I see this a-compositional idea as perhaps doing in traditional terms what very untraditional artists like Stella or Judd are doing in a very different way. I like these paintings best at the moment because they retain a certain sense of mystery even to me: I'm not quite sure what they're really about or why I do them. I think René Magritte as such a marvellous painter because his work is concerned with visual poetry at its purest. In his work the whole surrealist ideal of the domain of the marvellous coexisting with the 'real' world reaches its most beautiful and clear kind of realisation. Ernst, early Dalí, or Clovis Trouille have this kind of thing too but the great thing about Magritte is that he denies exegesis – you can describe the apparent content 'a woman's face made out of a woman's body', 'this enormous rock suspended over a landscape' without getting any nearer to the real meaning of the picture which is indescribable in words because it is conceived in purely visual terms. The statements are often philosophical ones which are nevertheless irreducible. This is the kind of pure painting that I'd really like to do. I think people assume too easily that purity involves abstraction (though it certainly did for Mondrian or Malevich) and don't see that other kinds of pure visual statements are possible. Some of the American realists like Andrew Wyeth, for example.

7. About Images

It's funny how often the word crops up when one is trying to talk about what one is doing. One also tends to use the word to describe a good shot or scene in a film for instance. When I organised an exhibition of young, post-pop painters some years ago I coined the phrase 'New Image' painting to describe their work. Poets like Arp, Lorca or Apollinaire work in terms of successions of images. Eliot's poems are cram-packed with them. What annoys me about 'The Movement's' poems, for instance, is that they tend to be a whole poem based on one image, rather like a weak Nescafé. Because I was trained as a painter I think my poems are concerned very much with concrete images, often visual ones. 'I Want to

Paint' is not about painting as such at all but a catalogue of ideal images without reference to media. In my early poems I tried to write 'traditional' modern poems with a beginning, middle and end. One day it occurred to me that they didn't work because of the way I got the raw material for them. I carry around a notebook and scribble down bits of things seen or ideas as they occur. It seemed to me much more honest to simply refine these, make them clearer, and then number them in sequence. These images were direct quotes of reality, usually in the sequence they occurred or the one that seemed most fitting. 'Liverpool Poems', 'Piccadilly Christmas Poems' and 'Wild West Poems' for example. I then realised that a lot of poets I admired like Pete Brown, Ferlinghetti or Ginsberg and earlier writers like Lorca or Whitman used a repeating or running phrase to link an image-sequence. Poems like 'Without You' were based on this. The problem here, as I remember Brown once saying, is that the image that follows must make the repeated word/phrase seem different each time, to avoid monotony. 'Tonight at Noon' and 'Mrs Albion...' are modified examples of this procedure. More recently in a poem like 'The Midnight Hour' I used the same 'catalogue' of images, but vary the sequence or speed by having each section with lines beginning with nouns, then participles, etc. Maybe I will be able to write poems with a beginning, middle and end one day.

8. As I said above, what fascinates me about art is the process of metamorphosis. This is why I think the new twentieth-century tradition of collage/assemblage so exciting. One thing I think is interesting about working today is a sort of awareness about how much personal content can go into a work of art and not violate its universal validity. 'The Large Glass' and some of Kienholz's tableaux are two very different examples of a *very* personal, almost esoteric content still being valid through the artist's power to externalise this content. As I suggested above, this is an almost purely 'formal', aesthetic problem. Another good reason for writing poems is that somehow they manage to get 'closer in' to one's own personality. It's interesting that an art student will show you his drawings but would be very shy about any poem he'd written, and asking to see them would be like asking him to expose himself. I think most people feel like this – I know I used to dread anyone reading my poems – they're somehow much more *personal*. I remember an interesting example of this with my poem-sequence called 'Love Poem'. This was originally written for and about Heather Holden. One copy was given to her and I kept the other.

One night I was stuck for something to read (a good thing about doing regular weekly readings is that they involve you in this kind of thing) and so I tried reading some sections of it leaving out our names. It seemed to go down well and *seemed* to mean something to other people. Then Brian Patten published it in *Underdog*. Since then I've discovered that even the most personal sections, 'Assemblage of objects and mementoes':

An almond with ALMOND written on it...
A red bra with I LOVE YOU written inside one of the cups...
A chocolate Easter egg... etc.

means something to most other people because nobody else has exchanged these
objects but everyone in love treasures some sort of small, meaningless mementoes
and recognises this quality if it's clearly and simply put.

9. Another interesting issue arises out of 'Love Poem'. In the 'Manchester Poem'
section there are a series of visionary evocations of people I admire in the context
of a love-affair in Manchester. Like:

Kurt Schwitters smiles as he picks up the two pink bus tickets we have just
thrown away

In a book review I once said that happenings consisted of what you couldn't
stick to a canvas – people, obviously, smells, perishable objects, places. In the
case quoted here poetry consists for me of a means to say something that it
would be impossible to paint: a recognisable Manchester street with someone
who was clearly Kurt Schwitters (let alone smiling – it's hard enough to paint
anyone smiling!) and no one else and anyway even if you could paint two pink bus
tickets convincingly to scale with the figure how could you make it clear they had
been thrown away by two people who had just walked out of the picture? It's like
primitive magic – to name something is to evoke its existence. Perhaps the nearest
I've got to doing this in painting is in the *Père Ubu* series and particularly in *The
Entry of Christ into Liverpool*. This has portraits of lots my friends and also various
heroes as well. None of the figures were done from life or photographs because
I wanted to paint the mental images I have of people – I nearly always think of a
particular person dressed in one set of clothes, for instance. It is also an elaborate
act of homage to James Ensor, who plays Christ. There is a quote from *The Entry
of Christ into Brussels* in the LONG LIVE SOCIALISM banner. And the 'Colman's
Mustard' advert is a quote from an Ensor drawing *Hail, Jesus, King of the Jews*
of 1885 which has I think the first bit of pop art in it. In the background there is a
poster for Colman's mustard. It is a kind of visual diary of the years it was painted
because the townscape was finished fairly quickly but the figures were done on
the additive principle for two years and sometimes I had to add beards or subtract
them or change the girls' hair colour or style. People I quarrelled with even got
painted out.

10. *About Entertainment*

The TLS reviewer who was so unhappy about *The Liverpool Scene* seized gratefully on Brian Patten saying: '... poetic entertainment is not poetry. It's not sort of big enough, you know.' This was rather like putting a hatchet into the hands of reviewers. I don't think that I work any less hard at writing a poem than other writers, or an essentially less serious. *But* having written the poem, then can it be more effectively presented in live performance? How would one read it? Can it be set to music or some kind of sound effect? Is there anything visual that can be added? If this makes one's work more accessible to more people without losing the quality of the work as written down then I'm prepared to take a chance of losing the support of Mr X of the TLS. That's why we always try to have music of some kind at readings – because music demands a different *kind* of listening than poetry and so provides a break. Even the most entertainingly presented poems become boring after an hour's uninterrupted listening. Programming, too, is important. Which poems to read in what order to suit the prevailing conditions. A good poem can be made to sound less good if put between two very similar ones. At the first big Albert Hall reading in 1965 it became obvious that the younger British poets (with one disastrous exception) had given some thought to which of their work would come across best under the rather peculiar conditions. The Americans, apart from Ferlinghetti, on the other hand, seemed to act as if it was a normal reading in a small room with forty people in it. When a lot of poets appear it is often a good idea to put them in some sort of order of contrast of qualities, just as one does in deciding what order to read poems in. I always start with a fairly 'entertainment' poem and then finish with a strong one. The ones between I try to vary according to content and mood. As the novelist Doc Humes once told me: 'An old vaudeville hoofer once said to me "Son, you don't follow one banjo act with another banjo act"'. All these considerations disappear, of course, when the poems are printed and read in solitude by someone else. This is the acid-test as far as the permanent values of one's work is concerned: does it have any meaning when not read aloud by the poet?

11. *A Note About Humour*

People tend to assume that writing poems that are funny is easy. This is by no means true. The one most obvious thing about jokes is that once you've heard them you know them. They lose their impact, which, as Freud says somewhere, arises basically from a power to shock. So if they don't work as poetry they don't work as humour after the first time. And re-reading them would be really painful. There is of course a lot of writing which is supposed to be non-serious but which is elevated (I think) to the status of literature: Lewis Carroll, Lear, Christian Morgenstern. I've always liked writers whose humour is basically verbal: the humour being in the words used rather than the situation described. *Alice in Wonderland* is one of my favourite books for this and many other reasons:

Thurber, Perelman and Wodehouse are masters of this verbal humour. I don't very often write deliberately funny poems: 'The New "Our Times"' is one of the few and that was hard to write because I wanted to catch the tone of Fénéon's original poem which is oddly solemn with all kinds of overtones, a kind of exaggerated black humour and vicious social comment, for instance. All presented as fact.

I wanted to retain this in a contemporary context which would be like the news on the telly or newspaper headlines. (Incidentally – there's a thesis subject going begging for some postgrad. student – 'The impact and influence of television on provincial writers'. Nobody in London will admit to ever watching the telly, leave alone being influenced by it.) Most of my poems have funny bits in them but are seldom all one mood. I like them to be a kind of emotional mixture which can be for instance serious and funny at the same time. I'd like to think that if you read through a dozen or so of my poems, which are mostly love poems, you'd be able to say what my views on most political or social or artistic questions were. I'd rather do it this way than write an overtly political poem or a straight love poem.

There was a lot of good funny poetry before 1939. Eliot is often very funny and I think he inspired writers like MacNeice and early Auden. This was completely killed off by the joyless ideas of the postwar movements. 'Bagpipe Music' is a very good poem as well as being funny. So is 'Letter to Lord Byron'. When I was writing an article about provincial artists and poets some time ago I discovered that most of them name as influences people dead or very old rather than fashionable contemporaries.

One thing about writing the kind of poems I write is that having a 'scene' helps enormously. If you have a regular audience they get turned on to what you're doing, they'll laugh at the funny bits and keep quiet for the bits that aren't, and enjoy the mixture. Liverpool people are amazingly good at this – by and large London audiences don't like this kind of thing because they tend to prejudge. A final aspect of this problem: as a painter I've always felt that one should eventually be able to make any kind of statement one wants to. A purely abstract one or a political one for instance. Even if this is only when you're very old, your technique and aesthetic should be both strong and flexible enough to allow any kind of statement that you really feel you ought to make. And I also think that modern art is largely autobiographical in origin. With someone like Picasso or Duchamp you can see how the various facets of their nature are reflected in their work. I have always felt I'd like to be able to walk around an exhibition and feel I'd know the artists quite well if I met him later. This is why the one-man show, the large retrospective or the monograph are vital today. Lawrence Gowing has pointed out how even artists like Vermeer and Cézanne who set out to efface any trace of personality from their work, by the very act of doing this set up a sort of peculiar emotional tension which gives their work its particular personal quality. The self-effacement can be as revealing as anything deliberately 'personal'. To get back to humour: I am a basically humorous kind of person, I think, and to write poems that are humourless because the weekly critics don't think it's literature would be denying a whole area of my experience and sensibility.

12. *About Mallarmé's Dictum*

One of the most important and fundamental statements about the function of a poet is Mallarmé's line *'donner un sens plus pur aux mots de la tribu'* which Eliot thought important enough to quote in one of his poems as 'to purify the dialect of the tribe'. This from someone who elevated poetry to the highest function of life, and pushed it furthest in the direction of an autonomous beauty unconnected with apparent meaning. To me the implications of this are obvious: to purify the dialect of *my* tribe. My tribe includes motorbike specialists, consultant gynaecologists, Beatles fans, the people who write 'Coronation Street', peeping toms, admen, in fact the language of anyone saying anything about anything in English. This implies the whole spectrum of specialist jargon, argot, dialect. More specifically I think my concern should be with the whole area of language as it impinges on me, now. Because we live in an era of communications-explosion, certain specialist uses of language seem particularly relevant: that of advertising (hoardings, slogans, TV ads) or newspaper headlines, where the aim is to transmit a message (or feeling) as quickly as perception allows, or that of pop songs or TV jingles where the basic aim is to establish a word/sound pattern in the memory as quickly as possible. Both demand considerable economy of means and a rethinking of ideas about syntax. In TV advertising, for example, a couple of extra words may cost hundreds of pounds.

Far from drawing away his coattails in disgust at the taint of 'commercialism' I can't help feeling that this new and different and economical use of language should be investigated by the poet. Not just imitated and quoted but considered as a repertory of possible devices. It is, incidentally, interesting that Mallarmé's line occurs in his 'Tombeau de E.A. Poe': Poe's theory of poetry has had little praise from English writers and yet events have largely borne out his reading of the situation: the 'lyric' is still dominant over the 'epic'; indeed it is hard to think of one good modern long poem which is not strung together lyric sections rather than a connected epic. I don't think that Marshall McLuhan's ideas necessarily invalidate the idea of a poet as 'purifier of the dialect of the tribe'. It seems to me that the whole post-Gutenberg galaxy of expanding communications *can* become the subject matter of the poet, it's just that most poets are afraid to face up to the consequences of it. It is another manifestation of a false concept of 'progress' to think that new media mean that old media have to go. Poetry, painting, sculpture and music-making in some form or other are constants in human society and will constantly reassert themselves. It was a commonplace around 1940 for writers like Herbert Read to say that easel painting as such had died out and that the whole idea of the fine artist would be replaced by the artist-architect-designer. They saw geometrical/biomorphic abstraction as the 'ne plus ultra' of modern art. What happened, of course, is now history. In Abstract Expressionism painting reasserted itself triumphantly, a totally unexpected manifestation coming from a totally unexpected quarter. Charles Olson's celebrated essay 'Projective Verse' can be read as a call to purify one's own dialect. The whole concept of writing for your own breath-and-speech measure is obviously conditioned by the kind of speech you hear around you from birth. This is what makes English 'beat' poets so hopeless: there are dozens of them still publishing in mimeographed magazines the same old poems written in mock-American. They follow the manner, not the spirit of the Americans. The great postwar revolution in American poetry consisted of writers like Kerouac and Ginsberg developing a new poetics and prosody by discovering their own voice, and recognising this quality in the practise of older writers like Olson and William Carlos Williams. But Williams' voice is not like Ginsberg's voice, nor like Creeley's. And so for a writer living in Liverpool and writing for his own voice and breath-measure the outcome will obviously be very different again.

13. The most specific formative influence on my thinking as a painter/poet was that of the 'Independent' group working in England in the late 1950s. Richard Hamilton was the most obvious influence although I didn't realise till some years later the implications of some of the things he had done at King's [College, Newcastle] with us. At the time I enjoyed them but couldn't really see the point. The group were interested in the theories of Ozenfant (*Foundations of Modern Art*), Moholy-Nagy (*Vision in Motion*) and other theorists but whereas *they* envisaged the future in terms of geometric abstract art, the Independents tried to relate the world of technological advance to the new world of conspicuous consumption and planned obsolescence. They postulated the idea of the artist as consumer. Lawrence Alloway proposed the idea of 'Pop Art' as a third category beside the traditional fine art/folk art dichotomy. The 'Pop Artist' is a highly conscious trained craftsman who designs objects for mass consumption. Detroit auto-stylists, record producers, photographers like Avedon and Penn come into this category. To the Independents the modern artist could choose from a whole range of styles and subjects from fine art and popular art to the mass 'pop' arts. To me the historical process involved in this attitude started the day Manet pinned up a Japanese print on his wall, or Bracquemond opened his shop. In England it began with Whistler's 'Peacock Room' and 'Farmer's and Roger's Oriental Warehouse'. Close upon this awareness of Oriental art came the revaluation of negro and 'primitive' art and the discoveries of archaeologists at Altamira and Lascaux. Suddenly the artist became aware that the post-Renaissance system of values was only one of dozens of possible alternatives all with their own value-systems. Worringer's 'Form of the Gothic' proposed a totally different system of evaluating the development of Western art in purely Northern, non-Renaissance terms. The codified systems of the post-Renaissance world, like Reynolds' 'Discourses', were no longer sacred texts. The Independents' great triumph was to point out that all other human

communications media beside the alternative traditions could be seen as equally viable activities. To the scientist a set of blueprints, a new horror film, *Woman's Own* and *The Waste Land* are all aspects of human communication. As with the surrealists perhaps the most important work the group did was ephemeral exhibitions like 'Man, Machine and Motion' (1955) and particularly 'This is Tomorrow' (1956). Some later exhibitions by apparently 'abstract' painters like William Green ('Erroll Flynn', 1959) and the Cambridge Group (1960) were interesting for what Alloway called 'Pop as Polemic and Affiliation'. What eventually became known as Pop Art in England was a sloppy, nostalgic and self-indulgent version of the ideas pioneered by the Independents.

Recently I saw a television interview with a distinguished American foreign correspondent. He had just come back from a tour of communist 'fringe' countries and he said the trouble was that young people everywhere wanted to grow their hair and play guitars. Be like other teenagers everywhere, in fact. He reckoned the 'Red Guard' fuss in China was an attempt by the leaders to keep the young people interested in the Revolution and away from this tendency. If this is so, (and it's certainly true of European communist countries) then the pop phenomenon may achieve what politicians have tried to do so often and failed. What is interesting too is the degree of freedom of expression the new pop stars have: I remember being at a party in Harrogate after a reading and Bob Dylan's *Blonde on Blonde* LP was playing; Adrian Mitchell was saying how good he thought the words were: I said, 'Yes, but isn't it amazing how much more freedom they have than we do'. What I meant was (and it's even more obvious with The Beatles' 'Sergeant Pepper' LP) that because of the whole pop aura that surrounds their work they could afford to allow themselves obscure or very personal images or sounds *and their public will accept it*. Whereas we always have to worry about the problem of communicating: what *can't* you allow yourself to say. I think this is a marvellous situation, for them. I think Dylan falls into the obvious trap this freedom opens, sometimes: The Beatles always seem to avoid it. Because no matter how interested in Oriental music or post-Stockhausen techniques they are they always seem aware of their responsibility as entertainers.

To return to pop artists in the 'Fine Art' sense of the word: to me the main requirement of the real Pop Artist (as distinct from the English 'Portobello Road' school) is a sense of history. The Pop Artist stands at the point of intersection of the history of aesthetics and the expanding communications-continuum of the modern world. The American Pop Artists since Jasper Johns have as their subject-matter the whole history of representation and communication, our accepted repertory of conventions for reality and illusion, not the hamburgers, pin-ups and packaging that are the ostensible excuse for the painting. Looking at Roy Lichtenstein's *WHAAM* in the Tate Gallery I was absolutely knocked out by the way in which, largely because of the size, the whole history of postwar painting was so obviously there: the variation in handling of the black lines between gestural and hard-edge; the edges of colour-areas soft like Rothko or hard like Newman; the colour stained in places into unprimed canvas and so on. I think in a much more minor sort of way that the same is true of my painting in that the direct influences on the way I work are much more from abstract painters like Pollock, Rothko, de Staël, Newman or Klein. As with poetry it is ultimately the formal values that determine its power as a permanent act of communication.

14. *Working notes for* Cake Painting No. 3 – *5 June 1967*
I'm not concerned particularly with literal truth, i.e. the exact number of currants on the bun... perhaps more the emotional truth... and certainly not metaphor – a circular Swedish pastry has more significance for me than a Mandala.

15. *The revaluation of the cliché*
This seems to me one of the most interesting aspects of what the Liverpool poets and some other young English poets are doing. The cliché is a living piece of language that has gone dead through overwork. At any time it can be energised or revitalised. Often by changing its context, putting it in an alien context, contradicting its apparent meaning. This applies equally to the visual arts: much of Dada/Surrealism and Pop Art consists of doing just this. Breton spoke of 'certain forms of association hitherto neglected': Lautréamont's 'beautiful as the unexpected meeting, on a dissecting table, of a sewing machine and an umbrella' is often highly quoted as a definition of surrealist procedures. Meret Oppenheim's *Fur-covered Cup, Saucer and Spoon* or Man Ray's *Cadeau* are perhaps the best-known examples of this process. In new English writing perhaps the most striking example of this revitalising process is the beginning of Pete Brown's 'Slam':

> They slammed the door in my face
> I opened the door in my face...

Often this occurs, as here, in the course of a long poem, but more often in a very short poem concerned with a single image or thought, a kind of subgenre, like Heather Holden's 'Still Life Poem':

> It might
> be nature morte
> but it's still
> life

or Roger McGough's:

> Your finger sadly
> Has a familiar ring about it

Pete Brown, Spike Hawkins and Adrian Mitchell are others who excel in this form. Many of McGough's dialogues use this destruction/rethinking of vocabulary as their basic progression. In my own case, I think 'Morning Poem', 'Drinking Song' or 'Winter Poem' work this way. Keith Arnatt, who is a very fine teacher and maker of constructions I used to work with, was interested in these little poems because he said they paralleled the sort of process involved in, say, the early work of Robert Morris and similar artists. Certainly in that they question common assumptions about language they are related to Swenson's idea of the 'Other Tradition'. The *Sergeant Pepper* LP by The Beatles has several lyrics that deal specifically with cliché ('She's Leaving Home', 'Good Morning'). Eliot once said somewhere that he thought 'television' was the ugliest word in the English language: someone, somewhere will come along one day and make it beautiful, I'm sure. In fact this does seem a rather self-contradictory statement because in his capacity as 'purifier of dialect' one major function of the poet must be as assimilator of neologisms. To me, the importance of Eliot's mature poetry lies in (1) his power of assimilating common speech, neologisms etc. This is what Wordsworth meant in the introduction to *Lyrical Ballads*. (2) In his awareness of new procedures in other art forms and the capacity to see their potential in poetry – like collage, montage or dissolve. And his awareness of other languages and literary traditions. (3) His special function was to marry all this to the 'Mandarin' tradition of symbolism which presupposed a 'pure' aesthetic. More recently, perhaps only in the novels of William Burroughs is there a similar power to weld these diverse aspects of language into a stylistic whole. In his introduction to *The Liverpool Scene*, Edward Lucie-Smith spoke of us as deriving from French poets the idea of the poem as 'agent' rather than 'object'. I must admit I hadn't *consciously* thought of it in quite these terms but it seems a very good way of putting it – certainly the concentration on related or contrasted images suggests this kind of basic concern, as perhaps particularly in my 'Poems Without Words'. To gain maximum impact the image must be as pure and clear and exact as possible. To me poetry must relate to everyday life and language, to common experience and shared assumptions, and yet provide 'the sound of surprise', the impact of something heard as if for the first time.

1   The same thing has been done with the present version.

From Collage to Happening: 'A Feel of Reality'

Catherine Marcangeli

Adrian Henri described himself as a 'notebook poet' who constantly jotted down ideas and impressions, people he had met, exhibitions visited, places discovered, situations experienced. He then turned some of this raw material into poems and pictures, often using collage as a structuring device. Those compositions explore the nature and status of images, visual and verbal, intimate and impersonal.

Collage and assemblage were also fitting media to respond to the disjointed experience of the modern city – fragments of magazines, newspaper headlines, logos, advertising material and found objects were thus used to depict and comment on the very world from which they were taken.

Henri developed and adapted the techniques of collage and assemblage into environments and happenings (or events) that invited the audience to be, not passive viewers, but actors in an unfamiliar participatory experience. This process was part of a strategy for drawing on the everyday as a means of narrowing the gap between art and life, and this essay focuses on several of Henri's key works from the early 1960s to the early 1970s – paintings, poems and performances – that share this approach.

Shopping for Images

Joyce Collage (1961) [Fig. 22] includes two pencil drawings of Henri's then wife, juxtaposed with small pieces of paper: a leaflet from an exhibition in London, a shopping list, a receipt from Lewis' department store in Liverpool, a bus ticket and an advertisement for Whiz which promises 'a brilliant new way of enjoying life'. These fragments are like biographical traces and attributes that arguably make the sitter more real, more present, and they are as much of a portrait as the artist's more traditional drawings of her. Although the fragments seem to have been juxtaposed arbitrarily, they are given graphic unity thanks to the name, 'Joyce', written large in black oil paint across them. The bold exclamation 'Go!' in the bottom-right corner balances out the composition, as does the tension between abstract marks (the dark purple patch, bottom-left) and commercial printed text ('Whiz!'). Just as in Picasso's collages, where the provenance and associations of words like 'ma jolie', 'bal' or 'journal' could give rise to biographical exegesis, so the viewer of Henri's painting is able to access autobiographical elements in the work. However, what gives this painting its quiet authority has more to do with its tonal coherence and formal qualities. Similarly, it is not the autobiographical or 'confessional' elements that make such love poems as 'Who?' or 'Without You'[1] effective, but the collage of evocative images linked, and given a rhythm by, the repetition of their title line:

> who
> wears my dressing gown
> and always leaves the sleeves turned up[2]

If readers are moved by the image, it is not out of sympathy for or because they identify with the jilted poet-persona, but because they recognise it as an image that has universal validity: it captures an intimacy of which every couple has its own version; it is the idea of the loss of such intimacy that one finds moving. Henri's images are often specific and personal, but their inclusion in a list or a collage depersonalises them:

> What fascinates me about art is the process of metamorphosis. This is why I think the new twentieth-century tradition of collage/assemblage is so exciting. One thing I think is interesting about working today is a sort of awareness about how much personal content can go into a work of art and not violate its universal validity.[3]

Through the 1960s, Henri produced variations on a list titled 'I Want to Paint'. An early manuscript pinned for a while to his studio wall read:

> I want to paint autumn hedges. Pain/the beginning of the dead year/poppy seeds briefly fertilised, turned up by the bulldozers of summer, blowing by motorways, torn away by the first wind of autumn, not to flower again/ hopes buried beneath dead leaves/first jade-dust of frost.

Although the list starts with an image that could indeed be painted – 'autumn hedges' – most of the others, paradoxically, could not. The expanded published version juxtaposes images that are just as impossible to paint, including:

> I want to paint
> The assassination of the entire Royal Family
> Enormous pictures of every pavingstone in Canning Street
> The Beatles composing a new National Anthem
> Brian Patten writing poems with a flamethrower on disused ferryboats
> A new cathedral 50 miles high made entirely of pram wheels[4]

As a painter and a poet, Henri explored ways of producing a 'catalogue of images', constantly questioning the forms he used.[5] When, for instance, does the scrapbook become a collage? During The Liverpool Scene's 1969 US tour, Henri collected a variety of items: newspaper and magazine cuttings, boarding passes, addresses written on the backs of envelopes, pieces of adhesive tape from 'U.S. Customs Montreal'. *New York Collage No. 6, Self-Portrait for Susan (with Hero)* (1969) [Fig. 63] includes a self-portrait taken in a photo booth, a hero sandwich (the name itself, let alone the image, must have seemed both Pop and surrealistic), a letter from the ICA, London, sent to Henri care of an address in New York, notes and observations, a guest pass for the Fillmore East rock venue.

As for *New York Collage No. 3, Homage to Robert Motherwell* (1969) [Fig. 62] it is an elegant abstract composition made from various paper bags picked up at The Museum of Modern Art where Henri had just seen Motherwell's paintings. Henri used some of these scraps of paper, together with photographs and ephemera, in a collage for the cover of The Liverpool Scene album *St Adrian Co, Broadway and 3rd* – whose first side was itself a continuous track titled 'Made in U.S.A'.[6]

The Liverpool Scene, *St Adrian Co, Broadway and 3rd*, RCA, 1970

Adrian Henri, *America, A Confidential Report to Dr Bertolt Brecht on the Present Condition of the United States of America* (London: Turret Books, 1972)

Also following the American tour, Henri published a book-length poem titled *America*. Presented as fragments from a travel journal, complete with locations and dates, *America* is a succession of images from that tour – 'soft ribbed sandclouds', landscapes from airplane windows, the noise of police sirens, advertising slogans, three prostitutes looking like the Supremes about to break into song, Joseph Cornell's *Taglioni's Jewel Casket,* floodlit skaters in Rockefeller

Plaza. One section is dedicated to Allen Ginsberg, who is described as Henri's 'stumbling walk guide to the nightworld' – just as Ginsberg himself had described Whitman as his own guide in the poem 'A Supermarket in California':

> What thoughts I have of you tonight, Walt Whitman, for I walked
> down the sidestreets under the trees with a headache self-conscious looking
> at the full moon.
> In my hungry fatigue, and shopping for images, I went into the neon
> fruit supermarket, dreaming of your enumerations![7]

In the collages, album track and book, Henri too is shopping for images and enumerations; each of the 'American Tour' works echoes the others, as well as numerous artworks, songs and poems from Henri's *Musée imaginaire* that are woven into their fabric.[8]

Polythenescapes

Collage enabled Henri to convey the urban experience. In the 1950s and 1960s, many British cities were turning into what he termed 'King-size polythenescapes'. Advertising leaflets, slogans and flashing signs thus found their way into his work. As early as 1956–57, *City Painting* incorporated commercial iconography, including a Weetabix logo, against a neon-lit cityscape in the style of Nicolas de Staël. One of the most formative influences on Henri's early work was Richard Hamilton and the Independent Group: from Hamilton's classes in Newcastle, Henri took away the notion of a continuum between high and low culture, and the idea that the artist must reflect, and reflect upon, changes occurring in her or his environment, including modern means of communication and advertising.

City Painting, 1956–57, mixed media on card, 28 × 19 cm

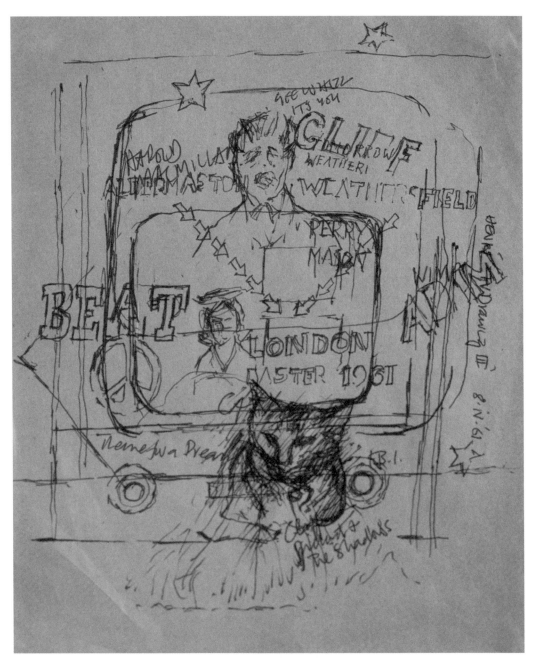

Adrian Henri, *TV Drawing III*, 1961, ink on paper, 22.5 × 16.65 cm

In his series of *TV Drawings* done over a few days while visiting his parents in Rhyl, Henri explored the bombardment of images into people's homes through the comparatively new medium of television. He sat in front of the twelve-inch set, sometimes with a cat on his lap, as in *TV Drawing III, 8-IV-1961*, and captured images and words as they appeared: a news item about the then British Prime Minister Harold Macmillan, the weather forecast ('tomorrow's weather'), mention of the anti-nuclear Aldermaston march of Easter 1961, in which Henri took part, and of the Weatherfield march, and a Campaign for Nuclear Disarmament peace sign. There are also references to popular culture: Beat, Perry Mason (the Los Angeles defence attorney in the CBS TV detective series), a portrait of Cliff Richard surrounded by stars and song titles – 'Gee Whizz it's You', 'Theme from a Dream' – and the caption 'Cliff Richard and the Shadows'.

Aldermaston March, 1961

The superimposition and juxtaposition of images and texts do not attempt, like in Cubism, to depict an object from several angles; rather, Henri renders the rapid succession of images and words, producing a kind of temporal Cubism, a collage of time instead of space. He approached writing in a similar way, urging poets to investigate and appropriate the language of the new media:

Because we live in an era of communications-explosion, certain specialist uses of language seem particularly relevant: that of advertising (hoardings, slogans, TV ads) or newspaper headlines, where the aim is to transmit a message (or feeling) as quickly as perception allows... a rethinking of ideas about syntax.[9]

In 'Man, Machine, Motion', the 1955 exhibition he curated at the ICA in London, Hamilton envisaged ways in which means of transport – aquatic, terrestrial, aerial and interplanetary – have transformed our perception of the spaces we inhabit. In his *TV Drawings*, Henri examined how the syntax of television transformed our relationship to time, and structured our perception of language and images.

Henri also explored how advertising was now 'structuring' and informing people's perception of the city. In the early 1960s, while teaching at Manchester Art College, he produced a series of drawings of that city's Piccadilly Gardens. At the time, the Gardens were slightly sunken so that looking up one would see Piccadilly Circus-style neon signs and flashing advertisements: 'Below eye level was grass. On eye level was the shops. Above eye level was the advertising. So that it had a layered feeling to it'.[10]

Henri celebrated the energy of the contemporary city, all the while savouring the ironic tension between nature and artifice: 'even the little bit of nature in Piccadilly was artificial. The flowerbeds were maintained by the Council. One day there would be a dense mass all of one colour, the next of another colour'.[11] In *Piccadilly Painting II* (1964) [Fig. 3], the bottom half of the picture consists in flat patches of colour: green for a notional grass, and yellow and pink for notional flowers. In the top part of the picture, the consumer goods include eggs and chips, a Mother's Pride slogan and adverts for Guinness and Bass. A bird – a recurring image in Henri's work – is painted against a 'kind of blue', a phrase that refers both to the paint, to the murkiness of the city sky and to the 1959 Miles Davis album to which Henri paid homage the following year in a series of collages [Figs. 58–60].

Further highlighting the artificiality of urban nature is the exclamation 'Daffodils are not real'. Thanks to Wordsworth's poem, the daffodil had long been emblematic of Romantic poetry, and of its epiphanic relationship to nature. Therefore Henri found it delightfully ironic that plastic daffodils should come as gifts in packets of Omo washing powder. They featured in several of his paintings as well as in early happenings, such as *Paintings, Daffodils, Milkbottles, Hats* and *Daffodil Story* (both 1963). For the latter, Henri and Brian Patten wrote a series of 'daffodil poems', recited and played back on tape. During the event, Henri painted a huge daffodil, live music was played by the local band The Undertakers, Wordsworth's poem was read out, and a caped Death figure distributed dead flowers to the audience.

Daffodils reappeared in one of Henri's most famous collaged poem: walking by chance past a motorcar showroom, he noticed an advertisement for a Dutch car, the DAF, marketed as 'The New, Fast Daffodil'; he picked up the leaflet, cut it up, cut up Wordsworth's poem and made a collage of the two texts. Unlike Tristan Tzara's recipe for a Dada poem – cutting up any text from a newspaper, putting the words in a bag, shaking it, and leaving the result up to chance – in Henri's poem the quotes from Wordsworth appear in the same order as in the original, for maximum effect: the reader, often familiar with 'The Daffodils' is tempted to complete the sentences, but is then wrong-footed by the DAF sales pitch:

Top: *Daffodil Story* event, Hope Hall, Liverpool, 1963
Bottom: *Paintings, Daffodils, Milkbottles, Hats* event organised with John Gorman and Roger McGough for the Merseyside Arts Festival, Hope Hall, Liverpool, 1963

I wandered lonely as
THE NEW, FAST DAFFODIL
FULLY AUTOMATIC
that floats on high o'er vales and hills
The Daffodil is generously dimensioned to accommodate four adult
passengers
10,000 saw I at a glance
Nodding their new anatomically shaped heads in sprightly dance
Beside the lake beneath the trees
in three bright modern colours
red, blue and pigskin
The Daffodil de luxe is equipped with a host of useful accessories
including windscreen wiper and washer with joint control
A Daffodil doubles the enjoyment of touring at home or abroad
in vacant or in pensive mood[12]

This variation on a canonical work is not a straight debunking parody – although
the poem had been drilled into Henri as a schoolboy, he was an admirer of
Wordsworth – but rather an ironic reflection on the contrasted registers that
could now coexist in the modern environment, a 'rethinking of ideas' about the
disjunctive syntax of high and low.

High and low, religious and commercial this time, are juxtaposed in *Our
Lady of the Detergent Packet* (1963) – anticipating Andy Warhol's *Raphael Madonna
$6.99* (1985), as well as the ironic association of godliness and cleanliness in
Warhol's *Last Supper* series from the 1980s, which combined Leonardo's famous
image with the General Electric logo (divine light metaphorically descending on
the scene) and the Dove soap logo (the dove/Holy Spirit flying in).

Adrian Henri, *Our Lady of the
Detergent Packet*, 1963, ink on paper,
35 × 27 cm

In the 1960s, like many artists of his generation, Henri was fascinated by an America that was enjoying push-button-age prosperity at a time when memories of ration books were only too fresh in English minds. However, he maintained a certain ironic distance. In his *Homage to Warhol*, the iconic Campbell's Soup logo is swapped for a quintessentially British variety, Heinz's Mulligatawny. Beyond the nod to Warhol, who was fast becoming America's most famous Pop artist, what interested Henri was the tension between abstraction and figuration: he used a real soup label, a fragment of reality collaged onto the picture, raising questions of appropriation versus creation, mechanical reproduction versus the unique work of art. Next to it, he painted a picture of that label, a hand-painted Pop image that works as a modern still life. Next to these is a gestural splash – Ed Ruscha-style soup – adding to the critical debates of the time by suggesting that abstraction and figuration were not necessarily irreconcilable.[13]

24 Collages No. 6, Mulligatawny Soup Painting (Homage to Andy Warhol), 1964, collage and paint on paper, 53 × 45.5 cm

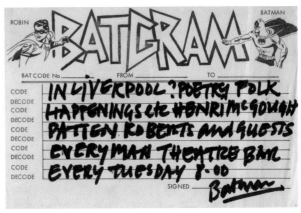

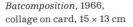

Batcomposition, 1966,
collage on card, 15 × 13 cm

Leaflet for *Batnight*, The Everyman Theatre,
Liverpool, 1967

Henri also drew on popular culture to make political points. The *Batman* series was broadcast on British television from 1966 to 1968, and Henri watched it regularly. He also bought several Batman cut-out books and sticker books, which he used in collages. Whereas his earlier collages usually contrasted and balanced abstract brushstrokes with printed images from magazines, his Batman works consisted only of cut-out figures from those books: the medium suited the subject.[14] *Batcomposition* (1967) [Fig. 40] is full of excitement and energy: the overall design explodes into its bright blue background, and the onomatopoeia add to the dynamism of the piece. Around that time, Henri, McGough, Patten and others organised 'Batnights', during which writers and musicians would perform Bat-themed sketches, songs and poems. As is made clear by badges Henri wore at the time, Batman and Robin were 'Against the Bomb' and his written homage to the superhero is much more ambivalent than his collages: the first stanza of 'Batpoem' (complete poem, page 16 above) starts like a celebration of popular culture and sexual liberation, but the second unexpectedly, and therefore all the more effectively, moves to an indictment of America's involvement in Vietnam – from the BatPill to BatNapalm.

Take me back to Gotham City
    Batman
Take me where the girls are pretty
    Batman
All those damsels in distress
Half-undressed or even less
The BatPill makes 'em all say Yes
    Batman

Help us out in Vietnam
    Batman
Help us drop that BatNapalm
    Batman
Help us bomb those jungle towns
Spreading pain and death around
Coke 'n' Candy wins them round
    Batman

In 'To Whom it May Concern', one of the strongest anti-Vietnam poems of the era, Adrian Mitchell denounced the war in an accusatory and defiant tone.[15] Here, Henri opted instead for irony, parody and sarcasm. He performed the poem to the upbeat theme tune of the television series, further underlining the jarring discrepancy between style and content, optimism and accusation.

Assemblages

Henri's Pop sensibility and aspiration to include reality into his works led him to incorporate 3D elements into some of his pictures. However, his assemblages often have a more deliberate narrative content than Robert Rauschenberg's *Combines* and are more formally composed than Allan Kaprow's *Rearrangeable Panels*. In Henri's *Liverpool 8 Four Seasons Painting* (1964) [Fig. 13], for example, several components are objects found by chance but that acquire a certain resonance when combined: because chrysanthemums are often placed on graves, the plastic flowers in the Autumn panel are associated with death; like the dead leaves Henri collected in the street, the flowers are fixed to the panel with paraffin and announce the approaching end of the year, and of life; juxtaposed with the pink heart, they also evoke the end of a love affair.[16] As for Summer and Winter,

> the cream and hard-edge shape is on the one hand a reference to hard-edge painting which was on the go at the time, and on the other hand it was the colours that the fairground at Rhyl was painted in. And then the little thing that looks like a bit off a spaceship is actually a lump off a fairground ride. It got broken off and was just lying around. (...) On the one hand it was simply about gathering up debris from the streets in Liverpool – things found lying in the gutter – a twisted pram wheel, a child's handbag and a child's teddy bear. Somehow or other when they were stuck onto the surface they seemed to be telling a story. It was almost like the idea of a street accident – a child had been run over. Again Winter is a bit like the Autumn picture – the silver was burying them as if it was something emotional or tragic that winter had covered up. The silver was slightly depersonalising the whole thing.[17]

As often, Henri plays with tensions – between hand-painted marks (the graffiti in Spring) and collage (the poster in Summer), between figuration (the depiction of a road in Spring) and abstraction (the same grey surface divided by a horizontal yellow line, like an abstract composition), between fake nature (the plastic daffodil and grass in Spring) and sophisticated artifice (the female model under a luxurious silk sheet in Summer), between sentimental evocations (the teddy bear in Winter) and hard-edge neutrality (the stripes of fairground colours in Summer).

Similarly, the composition of *Big Liverpool 8 Murder Painting* (1963) [Fig. 10] plays on textures and forms, but the found objects are also chosen because they bring with them a narrative potential: a newsstand poster announcing a court hearing for a murder case, a handbag, a pair of tights on which Henri splashed red paint and an advertising poster for John Courage beer all combine to suggest the remnants of a murder scene.

> I got carried away a little bit. I put a very used and grotty kind of lipstick into the handbag and a little bottle of cheap scent and a rather grubby little hanky. All these things which nobody would know about. In a gallery you wouldn't be allowed to look into the handbag anyway. They were just there to give it a feel of reality.[18]

'Nobody would know about' the victim's personal belongings, so the 'feel of reality' which Henri mentions would in theory only be perceived by himself and the few people who knew he had slipped the lipstick into the handbag. All the same, an ominous atmosphere arises from the picture, largely because the objects in the assemblage are real rather than depicted. In a 1964 event written and performed with Patten, the image resurfaces, described like successive close-ups from a film:

> Cold pavement
> crumpled stocking
> black handbag still smelling of lilies of the valley
> red pool slowly soaking into the gutter
> broken spectacles screaming silently for help[19]

A dark strand runs through Henri's assemblages, and his *Death of a Bird in the City* series likewise draws part of its effect from the presence of real objects. He started painting very gestural, almost calligraphic pictures of birds in the 1950s and returned to the subject throughout his career, referring to it in his poetry too – 'Without you white birds would wrench themselves free from my paintings and fly off dripping blood into the night'.[20] The image was derived from several sources: Henri remembers looking at a photo of a work on glass by Marcel Duchamp, 'photographed at night with lights below and odd shapes',[21] and mistakenly interpreting one of those shapes as a bird fluttering and about to die. Besides, he had just read Federico García Lorca's *Poet in New York*, which included 'a whole section on birds dying in cities' and made a lasting impression on him.[22] He associated those birds with people dying alone and isolated in big cities. John Gorman has suggested that the great number of birds killed by traffic also gave Henri the idea for his 1962 *Death of a Bird in the City* event (1962) [Fig. 14].[23] After the release of Alfred Hitchcock's *The Birds* (1963), the image took on additional resonances and associations.

Adrian Henri, *Bird Dying for its Country*, 1963-4, oil on board, 122 × 91.5 cm

In *Bird Dying for its Country* (1963–64), Henri makes a more specific political point: he explicitly connected this painting to the fiftieth anniversary of the outbreak of World War I by inscribing, under the British flag, a line from Horace that Wilfred Owen famously denounced in one of his poems: *'Dulce et decorum pro patria mori'* ('It is sweet and right to die for one's country').[24] The bird is emblematic of innocence lost in vain – 'the old Lie', as Owen called it – and the treatment of the picture surface echoes the violence of that sacrifice: Henri used a hot poker to scorch it, marking it as soldiers were marked by mustard gas burns. The link between war, birds and urban violence is also made in 'Death of a Bird in the City II', a poem dedicated to the war photographer Philip Jones Griffiths:

Guns are bombarding Piccadilly
Firing at ten million splattered white dying birds

Doors thrown open
Girls mouths screaming
The last unbearable white bird
Spotlit, slowly struggling threshing against blackness
Crucified on the easel[25]

In *Death of a Bird in the City* (1961), a bird is 'Crucified on the easel'. This stark picture includes a bent bicycle wheel and a stuffed sea bird whose neck has visibly been broken. By attaching real objects to canvas, to board or to a real door in the case of *Night Door (Homage to Djuna Barnes)* (1964–65), the artist went beyond the production of an image, however striking, and entered the viewer's space. These works place Henri in the tradition of assemblage, a practice that was given particular prominence in 1961 by the landmark exhibition *The Art of Assemblage* at The Museum of Modern Art in New York.[26] Yet their Christic or metaphorical content, and their titles, call for readings and interpretations that say as much about life as about art.

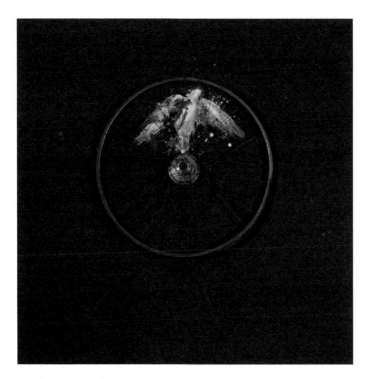

Death of a Bird in the City, 1961, oil on canvas with encaustic, stuffed bird and bicycle wheel, 120 × 120 cm

Environments and Happenings

As a student, Henri had become fascinated by the elegant poetry of Kurt Schwitters' collages and by the methodical and organic creation of the environment that was to become the *Merzbau*. Schwitters' adoption of the prefix *Merz-* to subsume all his activities, be it poetry, music or art, seemed to Henri the most apposite way of dismissing traditional categories: not only could the artist work in different media, but he or she could offer the viewer a more complete, multi-sensory experience – a total art.

When the Independent Group held the exhibition 'This is Tomorrow' at the Whitechapel Gallery in London in 1956, artists, architects, critics, graphic designers and musicians collaborated on composite environments. Group 2, comprising Hamilton, John Voelcker and John McHale, juxtaposed images from high art (a reproduction of Van Gogh's *Sunflowers*) and popular culture (posters of Marilyn Monroe and of Robby the Robot); a jukebox played music, while the sense of smell was stimulated by a carpet that released a strawberry scent when visitors walked on it. An Op Art-like corridor and rotoreliefs by Duchamp disrupted the visitor's spatial perceptions. 'This is Tomorrow' was a collective endeavour that addressed all the senses and invited the visitor to interact with the installation, yet it was different in tone from the effect Henri aspired to – it was very aware of design, more curatorially conceived and sociologically analytical of contemporary culture, whereas in the late 1950s and early 1960s Henri was increasingly attached to commonplace activities and ordinary spaces.

For example, his *Summer Poems Without Words* (1965) (see below, 208) were originally distributed to the audience in leaflet form. The list of instructions to be carried out 'over a period of seven days' included:

2. Travel on the Woodside Ferry with your eyes closed.
    Travel back with them open.
4. Find a plastic flower. Hold it up to the light.
5. Next time you see someone mowing a lawn, smell the smell
    of freshly cut grass.
8. Look at every poster you pass next time you're on a bus.
10. The next time you brush your teeth *think* about what you're doing.[27]

The fact that these instructions should be addressed to a 'you' emphasises the importance of the reader, viewer or audience – a direct consequence of Henri's activities on the live poetry scene in Liverpool since 1961, with McGough, Patten and others. Setting up readings and performing weekly in front of a (paying) audience made them acutely aware of the need to be accessible, and entertaining:

The poets (...) care about most of the things that our audience care about. We make as much effort to ensure their participation as possible – 'audience poems' made collectively are popular – and try to remove the barriers between performer and audience whenever possible. The predominantly teenage, non-intellectual, non-student audience like to laugh with McGough and cry with Patten about the sort of problems we all share. They must do – they pay good money to, every Monday, and keep coming back for more.[28]

At pubs and clubs like Sampson and Barlow or the Cavern , and at ad hoc performance spaces like Hope Hall, the poetry readings often had musical interludes or musical accompaniment. Many of these venues were only a short walk from each other, and from the Art College, making such collaborations all the easier and spontaneous.

Henri's collage-assemblage aesthetics soon extended into three dimensional interactive environments and happenings, considered as collages that unfolded in time as well as space. If that transition from collage to happenings was able to occur over such a short period, in 1962, it is undoubtedly due to the fact that collaborations between poets, musicians and artists were already commonplace. Henri's happenings should not be seen as different in nature from the rest of his œuvre. They were born out of his practice of collage, and of his public readings. Now, instead of juxtaposing fragments of images onto canvas, Henri turned a whole room into an environment in which to juxtapose moments, situations, fragments of the everyday, images, words, music, movements, actions and interactions with an audience: 'Happenings consisted of what you couldn't stick to a canvas – people, obviously, smells, perishable objects, places'.[29]

That approach to happenings was also influenced by Kaprow's writings.[30] Originally an abstract painter, the American artist became interested in the notion of environment after hearing John Cage's *4'33"* performed by David Tudor. During the 'silence', Kaprow realised that all the surrounding sounds – street noises, spectators' voices, the air conditioning – were indeed part of the piece, a found soundscape that blurred the boundary between the artwork and so-called real life.[31] For his 1957 *Action Collages* Kaprow produced movable panels, covered in electric light bulbs and artificial fruit and mirrors, whose configuration could be changed by the artist or viewer. At the Hansa Gallery in New York in 1958, visitors negotiated their way through strips of material suspended from the ceiling: they were both surrounded by and part of the environment. The same year, in an essay titled 'The Legacy of Jackson Pollock', Kaprow advocated in a somewhat prophetic tone the advent of a 'concrete art' that would reveal the world anew to both artists and audiences. That new art would involve all the senses and make use of everyday materials, such as:

> paint, chairs, food, electric and neon lights, smoke, water, old socks, a dog, movies, a thousand other things that will be discovered by the present generation of artists. Not only will these bold creators show us, as if for the

first time, the world we have always had about us but ignored, but they will disclose entirely unheard-of happenings and events, found in garbage cans, police files, hotel lobbies; seen in store windows and on the streets; and sensed in dreams and horrible accidents. An odor of crushed strawberries, a letter from a friend, or a billboard selling Drano; three taps on the front door, a scratch, a sigh, or a voice lecturing endlessly, a blinding staccato flash, a bowler hat – all will become materials for this new concrete art.[32]

Henri, too, had been using everyday materials, often collected or found in the street, in his collages and assemblages. For his first happening, fittingly called *City* [Figs. 4–8], he extended the urban environment to a whole room. The event was organised in 1962 as part of the Merseyside Arts Festival, which also included a parade through the streets of Liverpool, a debate on Apartheid chaired by George Melly between Bessie Braddock and Lord Lilford, art exhibitions and performances of music and poetry.

Programme for the Merseyside Arts Festival, Liverpool, 1962

The terms 'event' and 'happening' had both been used by Kaprow, but Henri settled on the former term, largely because at the time Liverpool shops were 'advertising sales as "Events": "Furniture event!", "50% Off Event!", "Discount Event!"'.[33] The idea of a 'Bargain Art Event' would have tickled Henri. Aware that the audience may have been disconcerted by this new art form, and always concerned they should not feel as if they were being talked down to, Henri and McGough produced a leaflet that acted both as a manifesto and as an explanatory introduction. The document outlines a background to the event, providing a lineage that ran from Dada and the Surrealists to the New York Assemblage painters, via Abstract Expressionism and jazz.

142

Henri's preparatory notes for *City* display all the characteristics of his 1960s events. *City* took place in a non traditional space, the basement of Hope Hall: built as the Hope Street Chapel in 1837, it had once been part of a chain of 'Continental Cinemas' and later became The Everyman Theatre. As the photographs of the event show, the space was intimate: Gorman recalls that it was 'rectangular … 15 × 30 meters … low ceiling … low light … low tech'.[34] The room was segmented by screens 'covered with hessian, brown paper, etc.' and a 'free-standing "junk" object'.[35] The set created and recreated fragments of an urban environment, including adverts and posters, newsstands, collaged magazines, graffiti, but also tapes playing city sound effects, street noises, sirens and traffic. During the event, painting, collage and assemblage activities were performed 'live'. Henri aimed to create an 'atmosphere through impressionistic tactile imagery adapted from the King-size polythenescape of which we in the city are all a part – (i.e. audiotactilism)'.[36] The piece did not attempt to tell a story, but to convey a city experience especially through the senses of touch, sight and hearing.

City was a collective work, a collaboration between different artists: the third column of his *First Notes* [Fig. 5] is titled 'cast', as if for a play, and mentions poets (Henri, McGough, Pete Brown), a painter (Henri) a photographer (Mike McCartney), as well as musicians, actors and an electrician. Poetry and music played an important part in the Liverpool events. In his 'Suggestions for Middle', Henri specified that Brown would read a section of his elegiac poem 'Night' accompanied live by 'any musicians available'. Live music by local bands was often supplemented with recorded music:[37] *City* for example closes on 'Folk Form No. 1', an appropriately fluid piece that unfolds around Mingus' bass rhythmic line.[38]

Roger McGough and Adrian Henri, *City* event organised with John Gorman and McGough for the Merseyside Arts Festival, Hope Hall, Liverpool, 1962

Staged in 1959 at the Reuben Gallery in New York, Kaprow's landmark *18 Happenings in 6 Parts* was precisely choreographed: audience members were given a set instructions on index cards, telling them where to sit, when they should stand, sweep the floor, climb a ladder, squeeze an orange, move to the next room, clap. A bell marked the beginning and end of each part:

> In contrast to Cage, whose encouragement of the participation of audience members was motivated by his desire to relinquish authorial control, audience members in many of Kaprow's happenings became props through which the artist's vision was executed.[39]

Kaprow's stage directions gave *18 Happenings* the look of a type of abstract theatre, directed by a tight score. In *City*, the audience was directed to a certain extent – the *First Notes* stipulate that the way in and the seated area were ' marked out in chalk on the floor' – yet the participants were mostly spectators of the performance. In later events, Henri and his collaborators devised ways of increasing audience involvement:

> The chairs for the audience were arranged in three groups, each facing different ways. The four corners of the room were four stages, each with a light and a microphone. The 'trick' was that the poetry and dialogue would be read in the different corners, forcing at least a third (sometimes all) of the audience to turn to see the readers. Sometimes the sound would be switched so that a reader would be in one corner and the sound would come from another corner. This was to make the audience aware of itself, and for the audience not to be taken for granted.

> Other event 'tricks' were (...) hanging varying lengths of string from the ceiling, causing the audience either to move them aside so that they could see, or to lean to see around the string (...) covering the seats in various materials, like polythene, to make people aware (...) giving the audience things to hold [such as] screws, sandpaper, wire.[40]

Like events by Cage or Kaprow, *City* was scripted – there was some room for chance, but even variations were anticipated on a page titled 'Suggestions for Incidents'.[41] This ensured that there would be no awkward lulls in the performance. Nor was it allowed to carry on indefinitely, as the music predetermined the duration of each segment – this gave a certain structure to a disparate piece that would have seemed otherwise chaotic. It would also have been reassuring for the audience to recognise some of the jazz or pop songs. Contrary to the relatively austere mood and self-conscious sophistication of Kaprow's happenings, humour was an essential ingredient of the Liverpool events, for the organisers were very aware that audience members must be entertained even while their assumptions were being challenged. Brown remembers the audience being a little bemused, 'but open-minded because they trusted the artists'.[42] The audience members were, after all, some of the same people who, drink in hand, were as likely to attend the Monday night poetry readings as concerts by local bands at the Cavern.

The set for *City* included a tarpaulin stretched over the audience's head and filled with advertising leaflets and posters, commercial packaging, soap flakes and other fragments of the everyday. At the end of the performance the tarpaulin gave way and the contents dropped onto the audience's heads – the 'tactilism' Henri referred to in his introduction. A newspaper journalist reported on the reaction: 'As the 60 invited guests came out, covered in soapflakes, chewing sweets and swapping bottle tops, they appeared to have enjoyed it' [Fig. 6]. Enjoyment, accessibility and inclusiveness were political imperatives for Henri, however experimental the art form.[43]

In a letter to Henri dated 5 September 1966 [Fig. 70], Kaprow remarked on the specificities of Henri's work in the UK, in particular his endeavours to create a collaborative intermedia work of art and his determination to use a specific locale:

> I've been hearing that London's so called vitality was a figment of our Time Magazine's publicity staff. The signals have been pointing instead to Liverpool.
>
> I think your idea of working with the local environment directly is important. The hard job is to gently sidestep the arty crowd and keep your big toes deep in the ground. It's hard because arty types seem to be supporters – they say nice things and give cash – but at bottom all they want is good taste and this is equated to fashion.[44]

From 1967, the success of *The Mersey Sound* and the demands of touring with The Liverpool Scene meant that Henri had less time to organise or take part in happenings. Following the break up of the band, he returned to the form in the 1970s, taking part in *Gifts to a City*, a project initiated by Wendy Harpe at Liverpool's Great Georges Project, known as The Blackie, 'a neighbourhood social and arts project in a poor, racially mixed area'.[45] As The Blackie's Summer Theatre for August 1971, *Gifts to a City* proposed a series of nine events, conceived as moments of surprise or double takes that interrupted the course of daily life. For 'Event 4' (15 August), photographs were taken of commuters on their way to work, of newspaper sellers or of people who did the same thing in the same place every day. The photographs were enlarged to life size and placed at night in the spot where they were taken – ready for the subjects to meet themselves coming back to work the next day. For 'Event 5' (16 August), passengers boarding the 6.07am bus from the city centre to the English Electric factory were told their fare had been paid, and were offered coffee or tea, a newspaper and a cigarette. In 'Event 7' (24 August), six large rectangular blocks made of 140 pieces of ice were erected on the Goree Piazza overnight for office workers to find in the morning. The twelve tons of ice, in a variation on Kaprow's *Fluids* (1967), were left to melt away.

'Event 9' (29 August) followed a script by Henri, titled *Six Memorials* [Figs. 20–1]. Unlike early events like *City*, which were very much *about* the urban experience, this performance took place *in* the city itself: six locations around Liverpool were marked with a white rectangle the size of a paving stone and six mourners laid a wreath in each and observed a minute's silence. With sites including the old 'Paddy's Market', the boarding point for the New Brighton Ferry and the Manchester Line ticket barrier at Central Station, the ritual memorialised familiar places, thus making them unfamiliar again.

It may seem curious that Henri, who extolled the Surrealists and the premium they placed on the imagination, should at the same time be so attached to the ordinariness and grittiness of the street. Yet what he found exciting in Jim Dine's *Car Crash*, Claes Oldenburg's *Street*, Ed Kienholz's *Beanery* or Rauschenberg's *Combines* was not a new sort of realism; nor did he consider the power of the imagination as some kind of Surrealist escapism. What he saw in both was the possibility of a revolutionary re-enchantment of the real: in much of his painting, poetry or performances, Henri strived not only to imitate 'the feel of reality', but to change the way reality feels.

Six Memorials, performance devised by Adrian Henri for The Blackie, Great Georges Project, Liverpool, August 1971

1   Adrian Henri, 'Without You', *The Mersey Sound*, ed. Edward Lucie-Smith (London: Penguin, 1967), 17.

2   Adrian Henri, 'Who', *The Mersey Sound*, ed. Edward Lucie-Smith, revised edition, (London: Penguin, 1983), 36.

3   Adrian Henri, 'Notes of Painting and Poetry', 115 in this volume. Interestingly, at the beginning of 'Without You', the pronoun 'I' appears five times in the space of a few lines, but then disappears from the poem to come back in the guise of a discreet and non-specific 'we'.

4   Henri, 'I want to paint', *The Mersey Sound* (1967), 51, and 10 in this volume.

5   Henri, 'Notes of Painting and Poetry', 114–15 in this volume.

6   The Liverpool Scene, *St Adrian Co, Broadway and 3rd*, RCA, 1970. The track 'Made in U.S.A.' juxtaposes texts written by Henri and Mike Evans.

7   Allen Ginsberg, 'A Supermarket in California' (lines 1–6) in *Howl and Other Poems* (San Francisco: City Lights Books, 1956).

8   On Henri's imaginary museum, see my 'Foreword' to the present volume.

9   Henri, 'Notes on Painting and Poetry', 119 in this volume.

10 Frank Milner, *Adrian Henri: Paintings 1953–1998*, (Liverpool: Walker Art Gallery, 2000), 56.

11 Ibid.

12 Henri, 'The New, Fast, Automatic Daffodils', *The Mersey Sound* (1967), 49. A pop group from Manchester active from 1988 to 1995 adopted the title of Henri's poem as their name: The New Fast Automatic Daffodils (later shortened to New FADS).

13 On the transition between Abstract Expressionism and Pop Art, see *Hand Painted Pop: American Art in Transition, 1955–1962*, ed. Russell Ferguson (Los Angeles/New York: Museum of Contemporary Art/Rizzoli, New York,1992).

14 Henri kept those books, minus the figures used in various collages. (See 'Material for collages' folder, Adrian Henri Archive, Estate of Adrian Henri, Liverpool).

15 Mitchell's poem, with its memorable repetition of the phrase 'Tell me lies about Vietnam' gained iconic status when it was read at the 'International Poetry Incarnation', Royal Albert Hall, London, 11 June 1965.

16 By contrast, the dead leaves in Kaprow's *Rearrangeable Panels* (1959) don't have as much of a metaphorical charge.

17 Henri interviewed by Frank Milner in *Adrian Henri: Paintings 1953–1998*, 69.

18 Ibid., 66. Henri added that 'When it was on show at the Walker, Brian Patten came to see it. He waited until none of the attendants were around and then he slipped a little poem into the handbag'.

19 *Night: a poem with and without words*, event written and performed by Adrian Henri and Brian Patten, Hope Hall, Liverpool, 1964.

20 Henri, 'Without You', *The Mersey Sound* (1967), 17.

21 Henri, interviewed by Milner in *Adrian Henri: Paintings 1953–1998*, 42.

22 Ibid, 44.

23 John Gorman, email to the author, 2 April 2014. In *Autobiography* (London: Jonathan Cape, 1971), Henri writes of birds 'Screaming white splattered against windscreen' and 'dying among bunches of nightblack flowers/painted screaming unheard in the tarmac city'.

24 Wilfred Owen, 'Dulce et decorum' (written in 1917–18), published posthumously, London: Chatto and Windus, 1921): 15.

25 Adrian Henri, 'Death of a Bird in the City (for Philip Jones Griffiths and his photographs)', in *Selected and Unpublished Poems*, ed. Catherine Marcangeli (Liverpool: Liverpool University Press, 2007), 106.

26 William C. Seitz, *The Art of Assemblage* (New York: The Museum of Modern Art, 1961).

27 Adrian Henri, 'Summer Poems Without Words', in *Tonight at Noon* (London: Rapp and Whiting, 1968), 31. Kaprow later turned one of those, brushing his teeth, into a performance 'activity' – see 'Art that Can't Be Art', in Allan Kaprow, *Essays on the Blurring of Art and Life* (Berkeley, Los Angeles, London: The University of California Press, 2003), 219–23.

28 Adrian Henri, 'The poet, the audience and non-communication' in *Sphinx*, Autumn, 1964, 27. The Monday readings Henri is referring to were the weekly readings organised under the banner of Patten's magazine, *Underdog*, at Sampson and Barlow's basement in London Road, Liverpool.

29   Henri, 'Notes on Painting and Poetry', 116 in this volume.

30   In *Environments and Happenings* – (London: Thames and Hudson, 1974), 117 – Henri remembers reading an article by Kaprow in early 1962. However, he had known of the American artist's work since at least 1961, as he mentioned him at a meeting of the Merseyside Arts Festival that year. The two artists started corresponding in 1966, and Kaprow went on to send Henri posters and scripts of his happenings into the 1970s ('Kaprow' folder, Adrian Henri Archive, Estate of Adrian Henri, Liverpool).

31   On his experience of hearing Cage's *4'33"* at Carnegie Hall in New York in 1952, and of seeing Rauschenberg's *White Paintings*, see Allan Kaprow, quoted in Joan Marter, 'The Forgotten Legacy: Happenings, Pop Art and Fluxus at Rutgers University', in *Off Limits, Rutgers University and the Avant-Garde 1957–1963*, ed. Joan Marter (Newark: Rutgers University and Newark Museum, 1999), 5. Kaprow attended Cage's classes at The New School of Social Research in New York in 1957–58.

32   Allan Kaprow, 'The Legacy of Jackson Pollock', in *Art News*, 6 October, 1958, 24–26, 55–57. Henri was also aware of Kaprow's article 'Happenings in the New York Art Scene', in *Art News*, 3 May, 1961, 36–39, 58–62.

33   John Gorman, interview with the author, Liverpool, 15 March 2014.

34   Ibid.

35   Adrian Henri, 'First Notes for "City" Event' ('City' folder, Adrian Henri Archive, Estate of Adrian Henri, Liverpool). Kaprow often used the term 'junk' to insist on the ordinariness of the materials to be used in happenings.

36   Adrian Henri and Roger McGough, *City Event: An Introduction* (Adrian Henri Archive, Estate of Adrian Henri, Liverpool).

37   Mike Evans in his sleeve notes for *The Amazing Adventures of...* (Cherry Red, 2009) explains that early happenings largely used recorded music, while later ones involved Liverpool bands such as The Undertakers, The Clayton Squares or The Roadrunners.

38   From the album *Charles Mingus Presents Charles Mingus (New York:* Candid, 1960).

39   Paul Schimmel, 'Leap into the Void: Performance and the Object', in *Out of Actions: between performance and the object, 1949–1979* (Los Angeles: Museum of Contemporary Art, 1998), 61.

40   Gorman, email to the author, 2 April 2014.

41   'City' folder, Adrian Henri Archive, Estate of Adrian Henri, Liverpool.

42   Pete Brown, interview with the author, London, 19 May 2014.

43   See Adrian Henri, 'The Poet, the Audience and Non-Communication', *Sphinx*, 27. Not surprisingly, the script for Henri's 1966 *Spring/Summer Event* closes with the stage direction: 'Event ends in dancing'.

44   'Kaprow' folder, Adrian Henri Archive, Estate of Adrian Henri, Liverpool.

45   Henri, *Environments and Happenings*, 117.

The innovation of easel painting made great works of art possible, but it has now lost this power. The cinema and the illustrated weekly have succeeded it.

Lissitzky

DESCENT

No one can escape from DADA
Only DADA can enable you to escape from destiny.

Tzara

INTO

. . . . remember that for us in this day and age it is reality itself which is at stake. How can we be expected to content ourselves with the fugitive complexity brought to us by such and such a work of art ?

Breton

THE

Now, as art becomes less art, it takes on philosophy's early role as critique of life.

Kaprow

STREET

We seek a form of action which transcends the separation between art and politics: it is the act of revolution.

Black Mask

Descent into the Street, from Henri's poster collection, late 1960s

In Local News: Adrian Henri's Total Art

Antony Hudek

As the novelist Doc Humes once told me: 'An old vaudeville hoofer once
said to me "Son, you don't follow one banjo act with another banjo act"'.[1]

The fate of Adrian Henri's reputation as a radical poet, painter and performer can
be mapped onto Liverpool's own fortunes, from its cultural heyday in the 1960s to
its pronounced economic decline in the 1970s and 1980s, and to its recent efforts
to regenerate itself as a cultural hub. As the exhibition of which this publication is
a trace and companion testifies,[2] Henri is ripe for reappraisal. But like Liverpool,
which now promotes itself on two fronts, as hip and cutting-edge as well as steadfast
and tradition-bound,[3] a contemporary return to Henri's art may go two ways:
lionising one of the great British performer-poets of the 1960s, or underscoring
Henri's intimate and unabashed attachment to Liverpool, making him, foremost,
a local phenomenon.

    In what follows I will interweave these two forms of historical return, and
suggest that it is through the latter (Henri as a local protagonist) that one most
readily arrives at the former (Henri as a key figure in international histories of
poetry-performance). The risk, of course, is that one may end up with yet another
eulogy of Liverpool's former centrality and continued relevance – in the (presumed)
words of Allen Ginsberg, Liverpool as 'the centre of the consciousness of the human
universe'[4] – an unmistakable symptom of a lingering cultural and economic
inferiority complex. Yet what I hope to find in this 'localisation' of Henri's creative
work, particularly in his book *Total Art* from 1974, is a means, more broadly, of
thinking the fabrication of performance history differently, that is, of 'reclaiming'
Henri not so much for his achievements in poetry, painting and performance as
for his methodological and historiographic radicalism.

    Besides the thematic strands that informed the exhibition as well as this book –
'city', 'love', 'heroes' and 'America' – I draw much of my information from a site that I
was fortunate to experience first hand: Henri's former home in Liverpool's so-called
Georgian quarter, and more specifically his ground-floor study. Thanks to Catherine
Marcangeli's steadfast efforts to preserve Henri's home and archives, the artist's book
collection has remained remarkably intact since his death in 2000. The layout of
the books lining the walls of the study shed valuable light not only on Henri's reading
preferences, but also on his connections to a wide network of international artists
and authors, many of whom (Ginsberg, but also William Burroughs and Allan
Kaprow, among others) he was in personal and sustained correspondence with.
Henri's book collection may be seen as a microcosm of his home, itself a paradigm
of his creative outlook: his view onto the world was broad, and the international
news he consumed and produced filtered by the local.

    What could be considered metaphors for Henri's method, his home contains
a number of wall-mounted wooden display cabinets, each containing a motley
assortment of Victoriana, trinkets and souvenirs – as if Joseph Cornell were let
loose in a car boot sale:

on the mantel piece 29 Grove Park
off Lodge Lane Liverpool 8
15th September 1966

(...)

1 postcard 'In the Forest'
by Douanier Rousseau
1 postcard of a Dubuffet mindscape
my keys to her flat
leather purse
Rentbook with 21 weeks paid
a fountain pen (black)
small Tupperware container
with 7 shillings for the gasfire
tube of Anadin (7 left)[5]

This casual elegance paired with the kitsch of personal mementos and souvenirs
may provide a key to Henri's aesthetic, which often interrupts the eloquent and
high-minded with discrepant fragments from the everyday. It also characterises
his book collection, with its accumulation of the rare (signed first editions) and the
common (Sunday supplements, comic books). It is important to note that Henri's
library constitutes a working collection, a research tool for his writing, and not a
hobbyist's enterprise; nor can it be simply interpreted as a subjective portrait of
the artist-as-reader: a library left behind after the artist's death will inevitably,
however organised (and Henri's is relatively systematic), miss the bibliographic
key to decipher it and its omissions and idiosyncrasies, namely the artist him/
herself.[6] Still, perusing the shelves in Henri's study gives one a sense of the
breadth of his intellectual panorama. When Walter Benjamin chose to describe his
own collection of books, he was giving clues to his ways of writing: his pursuit of
rare nineteenth-century French novels and early German children's books betray
a desire to craft a new form of writing history, at once novelistic, colourful and
aphoristic.[7] Henri's collection differs from Benjamin's bibliophilic intensity, yet its
strong holdings in Beat literature and historical eclecticism – from Surrealism to
contemporary art – suggest an equally distinctive methodology and style: one that
wanders discursively, or as Kaprow described his choice of illustrations for his
1966 book on happenings, one that would encourage 'reverie'.[8]

A Beat sensibility in Henri's poetry is hard to miss, especially in the ease
with which it lends itself to being set to music and performed. Strongly influenced
by jazz, Beat writing was not only meant to be read but read out loud – acted out –
publicly, in venues as varied as music clubs and art galleries. Ginsberg's poem
Howl was first performed on 7 October 1955 in an art space in San Francisco, the

Adrian Henri's study, Liverpool

Six Gallery, known for hosting some of the earliest proto-happenings on the West Coast. Both the Six Gallery, which operated from 1954 and 1957, and the King Ubu Gallery, another San Francisco gallery active between 1952 and 1954, aimed at creating a setting for 'total art' inspired by Dada by hosting events combining jazz, painting, light-shows, film and, not least, poetry.[9]

Although Henri's writings do not refer to West Coast performance as much as to East Coast artists such as Kaprow, Claes Oldenburg and Jim Dine, his description of his own events[10] as similar to 'Jazz Canto or Poetry & Jazz' affiliates him more to Beat than to New York happenings.[11] Much like the poetry produced in San Francisco in the 1950s, 1960s Liverpool verse was indebted to orality, drawing on the rich dialects and accents in the city and its surroundings, and to aurality, marked by the city's strong popular musical culture.[12] It is certainly no coincidence that the fifth title in the series of Penguin Modern Poets brought together poems by Gregory Corso, Lawrence Ferlinghetti and Ginsberg in 1963, four years before *The Mersey Sound*, with Roger McGough, Brian Patten and Henri, appeared as number 10 in the same series. The itinerant, vagrant quality of the writings of

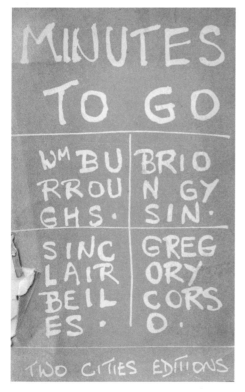 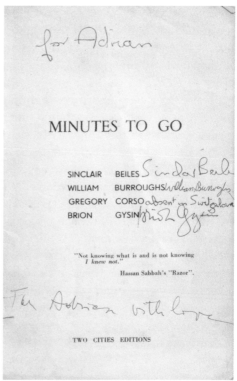

Sinclair Beiles, William Burroughs, Gregory Corso, Brion Gysin, *Minutes to Go*
(Paris: Two Cities Editions, 1960), signed by the authors 'For Adrian with love'

154

Jack Kerouac and Burroughs can be found in Henri's autobiographical sketches of his early years, in which he describes his moves from Birkenhead (where he was born) to North Wales (where he grew up) to Newcastle (where he studied fine art under Lawrence Gowing, Roger de Grey, Richard Hamilton and Victor Pasmore[13]) and back to Liverpool where he resided from 1957 to the end of his life. A particularly significant early biographical episode was his work on the fairgrounds of the seaside town of Rhyl, where he manned rides and stands during several summers. In his recollections of the heady atmosphere of the fair and the euphoria of the screaming customers as he played with the speeds of the rides,[14] one detects early attachments to the thrills of the young, especially of working class youth, as well as to the kitsch aesthetic abundant in many British seaside towns in summer.[15]

Adrian Henri, Roger McGough, Brian Patten, *The Mersey Sound* (London: Penguin, 1967)

A familiar trope for many artists seeking a liminal, carnivalesque and eroticised space,[16] the fairground must have inspired Henri's event-based works, where a lack of structure was compensated by the energy and spontaneity of the performances: 'There really was something there', wrote John Willett of Henri's 1963 event in Hope Hall cinema; 'Staging was poor, owing partly to amateurishness, partly to unsuitability of the stage; but there were no awkward lulls. And it was spontaneous, unpretentious, I thought, and above all indigenous'.[17] Willett himself made the connection between the faux-glamour and rowdiness of fairs and Henri's formative summers: Henri is 'above all, perhaps, a showman, for he has worked six or seven summers in a fairground at Rhyl (for which he has painted decorative panels), and he has a rare gift in an age of exhibitions of being able and anxious to present other people's work besides his own'.[18]

The positive showmanship in Willett's account would become expressly negative in the eyes of contemporary observers such as David Harsent and Paul Overy. Harsent, writing in *The Guardian*, disparaged what he saw as the Liverpool poets' 'fetchingly bittersweet cabaret turn'.[19] Overy singled out Henri as the prime culprit for this downward spiral in taste: 'What is happening in Liverpool is that attempts are being made to bridge the gap between art and popular entertainment, to get away from civic worthiness and art that looks down on people from pedestals and the walls of municipal buildings. Much of the work is frankly mediocre... The poet and painter Adrian Henri is a more sophisticated showman than [the Liverpool sculptor Arthur] Dooley, although it might be said of him... that he belongs more to the history of publicity than to the history of art'.[20]

Overy's negative stance towards Henri's showmanship owes as much to the critic's aesthetic preferences as to the difficulty in squaring Henri's hybrid events from the early 1960s with 'the history of art', a history in the UK that had yet to engage with happenings and performances. In 1965, in one of the first and most quoted studies of happenings (about which Henri wrote 'it is impossible to say how important this book is'[21]) Michael Kirby established a strong connection between happenings and theatre: 'Although some of their advocates claim they are not, Happenings, like musicals and plays, are a form of theatre. Happenings are a new form of theatre, just as collage is a new form of visual art'.[22] Unlike theatre, however, happenings suffered from what Kirby calls 'distortions', because such events were witnessed by very small numbers and seldom re-performed, in part due to their low-budget production values ('Happenings have had in common a physical crudeness and roughness that frequently trod an uncomfortable borderline between the genuinely primitive and the merely amateurish'[23]).

Outside of the few groups of artists engaged with happenings in the late 1950s and early 1960s, the form could have easily seemed a short-lived fad, which is precisely how the American critic Richard Kostelanetz saw it in 1965. Five years later, in his book *The Theatre of Mixed Means*, Kostelanetz recanted his judgment, placing the blame for his earlier shortsightedness on his decision 'to split the critical work into categories – cinema, fiction, dance, poetry, painting, theatre, and music'. Kostelanetz goes on to write that back in 1965 he was 'only dimly aware that so much that is currently artistically advanced today straddles, if not transcends, these traditional divisions'.[24] By the time of his 1970 revision, Kostelanetz had come around to Kirby's association of happenings to theatre; but he goes further, comparing them to early twentieth-century vaudeville: as 'a hybrid, mixed-means format that could encompass nearly every known kind of entertainment', the performance-based art of the 1960s 'is not exclusive but inclusive, exploiting everything it can potentially encompass, rather than putting down some feasible possibilities as beneath its dignity'.[25]

Around 1960, happenings in New York had unabashedly embraced their low-art status, with such performances as Kaprow's *The Big Laugh*, Dick Higgins' *Edifices, Cabarets, Contributions* and Dine's *Vaudeville Collage*, alluding through outlandish costume, props and facial paint to the spectacular but dingy world of the side show and road show.[26] A signal moment in this early history of happenings is 'Ray Gun Spex', the series of events organised by Oldenburg in 1960 at the Judson Memorial Church in New York, with performances by him, Dine, Al Hansen, Higgins, Kaprow and Robert Whitman. 'Spex' in the title means 'burlesque' in Swedish (Oldenburg's native language), an apt characterisation for many of the happenings in the series, particularly Oldenburg's own *Snapshots from the City*, which took place in an environment he created a month before, entitled *The Street*:

> *The Street* was a jumble of two-dimensional, silhouetted figures and objects whose ragged, blackened contours and monochrome brown-black tones reeked of the decay and brutality of life in the Lower East Side slimes. Oldenburg invited the audience to add its own debris to the floor of *The Street*...[27]

Happening artists like Dine and Oldenburg would soon start making much cleaner and commercially viable environments, which in turn yielded to displays of sellable art objects under the new denomination of 'Pop art'. Even Kaprow, though committed to time-based art and averse to object-making, bemoaned in 1965 the perpetuation in happenings of an aesthetic that 'smacked of night club acts, side shows, cock fights and bunkhouse skits'.[28] Henri, on the other hand, would remain attached to this early moment in the formulation of happenings, when crude scenography combined with semi-scripted, mostly musical performances inspired by their immediate urban context as well as by traditions of cabaret and vaudeville. He made his admiration for this aesthetic explicit by dedicating one of his poems to Dine's 1960 happening *Car Crash*.[29] For Henri, events were decidedly '*not* theatre', but 'a dramatic/humourous ritual happening aimed at working directly on the consciousness of those experiencing it'.[30] Whereas the commercialisation of American happenings resulted, according to Henri, in a 'phasing out' of the audience element, 'the new English performance artists had made a real breakthrough to a non-cultural audience: pop festivals, summer play schemes, work in the streets or in pubs'.[31]

Lacking an early 1960s local happenings scene to which to refer, Henri's event-based art, indebted to the inclusive atmosphere of vaudeville and fairs, has often been subsumed, erroneously, under Pop art. His salad and meat paintings from 1965 to 1971 [for example, Fig. 16] are undeniably 'Pop' in appearance, showing similarities with contemporary works by the likes of Wayne Thiebaud and Dine.[32] Even the figure of Ubu, not long before the privileged domain of experimental theatre and a recurrent character in Henri's painting, poetry and performance from the early 1960s, had by 1966 been co-opted by mainstream art, including Pop Art.[33]

In any case, 'Pop' in the context of Liverpool needs to encompass not only art, but popular culture generally, and pop music in particular. There is debate about the extent of the crossovers between Liverpool's poetry, art and music scenes: Jeff Nuttall has contended that The Beatles borrowed, consciously or not, from the city's pop art and happenings, while others have argued that the city's poetry and pop music developed in tandem but separately.[34] What is clear, however, is that 'pop' in Liverpool belonged more to music than to art: as Edward Lucie-Smith observes, 'Pop art is, at its most typical, full of ironies and subterfuges. Pop music, on the other hand, is dedicated to directness'.[35] Henri's proximity to the latter over the former put him on a divergent path from British Pop Art in the wake of his former tutor Richard Hamilton; instead, what attracted him in Pop was more an overall sensibility, a freedom to adopt styles and apply them to the canvas or stage in disregard of the teleological progression of modern movements as dictated by medium-specific, that is, modernist, histories of art. As Henri stated, 'suddenly the artist became aware that the post-Renaissance system of values was only one of dozens of possible alternatives, all with their own value-systems'.[36] The events that Henri staged from the early 1960s through the 1970s are further demonstrations of the artist's inalienable right to generate alternatives to any singular history of art, hybrid events mixing not so much mediums as stories.

Thus ostensibly a poet, painter and musician-performer, Henri aspired to the condition of total artist. 'Total Art' is the phrase he used as the title for the American edition of his survey of environments, happenings and performance published in 1974 by Thames and Hudson. Henri's choice of title is significant on three counts, each one positioning event-based art practices within older, rather than more recent, artistic traditions. First, 'total art' situates the origin of happenings and performance in a dramatic, indeed operatic tradition of Richard Wagner's *Gesamtkunstwerk*, 'the idea of something that partakes of all the arts'.[37] Second, the significance of 'total art' for Henri is due to the concept's embrace by Dada and Surrealism in the first decades of the twentieth century.[38] Finally, the phrase 'total art' betrays Henri's preference for the early phase of happenings at the turn of the 1960s, before their relative embrace by mainstream galleries and museums – while at the same time solving the persistent problem of what to call happenings and other event-based art.[39]

Establishing this pedigree of total art enabled the art actions Henri was interested in, including his own, to qualify as, if not acquire, official art historical status. Moreover, the expression's European roots allowed the emerging history of event-based art to take into account such movements as Actionism in Austria and Fluxus in France and Germany. In 1962, the French Fluxus artist Ben Vautier

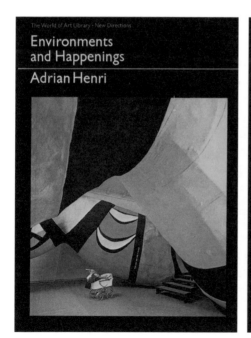
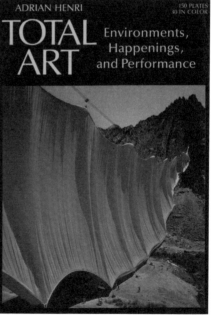

Left: Adrian Henri, *Environments and Happenings* (London: Thames & Hudson, 1974)
Right: Adrian Henri, *Total Art: Environments, Happenings and Performance* (New York, Toronto: Oxford University Press [under copyright of Thames & Hudson], 1974)

published an assortment of texts and small objects under the title *Art Total*.[40] Wolf Vostell, one of the earliest creators of happenings in Germany – which he referred to as '*décollages*' – similarly sought to create 'total works of art' or *Gesamtkunstwerke*.[41] In 1965 he co-authored with Jürgen Becker the book *Happenings: Fluxus, Pop Art, Nouveau Réalisme*, which tried to bring order to the numerous and often contradictory forms of event-based work taking place in Europe and North America at the time. As would soon become customary for survey publications on happenings, Vostell's and Becker's follows a chronological structure, beginning with the year 1958, the date of Allan Kaprow's untitled happening, Jean Tinguely's *First Concert for 7 Pictures* and a publication by the Zero group in Düsseldorf. The following year, in Vostell's and Becker's book, sees the official double 'birth' of the happening: Kaprow's *18 Happenings in 6 Parts* at the Reuben Gallery in New York and Vostell's own *TV-dé-Collage* in Cologne.[42] This dual origin – shared between the US (that is, New York) and Europe (primarily France and Germany) – would impose itself as the accepted historical narrative, in part thanks to the influential curator Harald Szeemann's exhibition 'Happenings and Fluxus' at the Cologne Kunstverein in 1970.[43] Szeemann explictly credits Vostell's and Becker's book as the inspiration for his exhibition, and naturally rehearses the double origin of happenings, beginning his own chronology in 1959 with, among others, the same two events by Vostell and Kaprow.[44]

Kaprow's own version of the history of happenings – *Assemblage, Environments & Happenings*, published in 1966 – unsurprisingly emphasises his own role in the early formulations of the genre. Interestingly, however, Kaprow also foregrounds the international character of happenings, by citing examples of Gutai 'Theater Art' from the mid- to late 1950s, and going on to list events by French artist Jean-Jacques Lebel (such as the latter's 1960 performance *Funeral Ceremony of the Anti-Process*), Vostell, George Brecht, Kenneth Dewey and Milan Knížák. 'In contrast to the increasingly homogenised character of the conventional forms of international creativity', Kaprow writes, 'the Happenings, I am glad to say, are distinct, both regionally and personally'.[45] Of all the surveys quoted above, Kaprow's book had the greatest influence on Henri's *Total Art*, precisely, one suspects, for its regionalism and unorthodox composition. As both writer and designer of the book, Kaprow divided it evenly between a section of photographic documentation of mainly US-based happenings and another of scenarios of international happenings. Among the photographs reproduced in the first part, Kaprow included only one of a 'historical' performance – Clarence Schmidt's untitled environment from 1930 – which is one of the main precedents of happenings illustrated in *Total Art*. Other photographs included by Kaprow, such as Vostell's *Nine Décollages* from 1963, also re-appear in Henri's book.[46]

Nevertheless, in one respect the histories of happenings put forth by Vostell/ Becker, Kaprow and Szeemann all seem to agree: British performance-based art played a trivial part in the emergence of the new art form. When it does appear, for example in Vostell's and Becker's chronology, it does so only tangentially, in 1962, with the Fluxus *Festival of Misfits* held at Gallery One and the ICA in London. Because the Vostell/Becker book came out in 1965, it could not have accounted for the later landmark British performance event, the Destruction in Art Symposium (DIAS) in September 1966, during which international Fluxus and happenings artists joined their London-based peers, including Ivor Davis, John Latham and Gustav Metzger. Szeemann's 1970 exhibition and publication did refer to DIAS, as well as to a concert held at the ICA in November 1965, in which Metzger and US artists Higgins and Alison Knowles took part. But aside from these few events, no other UK-based manifestation makes the cut in these early international surveys. The oversight is hardly unique – important Polish and Brazilian happenings, to name a few, receive equally scant treatment – but it has had a lasting and deleterious effect on histories of 1960s event-based art in the UK, which have only recently begun to attract the attention they deserve. It is telling, for example, that the author of a recent study of American happenings from the 1950s and 1960s, in which Kaprow holds the leading role, would regret the fact that 'to date no scholar has successfully untangled happenings from theatre (or from performance art), nor has any art historian attempted to tackle the issue'.[47] If North American scholars can deplore the lack of serious attention paid to US histories of happenings, one can only guess at how much work still needs to be done to produce a detailed picture of happenings and performance art in the UK from the early 1960s to the late 1970s.

Heike Roms and Rebecca Edwards have recently suggested that the lack of a British history of happenings is due to the fact that this art form has 'few distinctive – or distinctively "British" – traits'.[48] This may be true when compared to the unalloyed British Pre-Raphaelite and Arts & Crafts movements, yet one would have difficulty identifying what makes Kaprow's, Whitman's or Oldenburg's New York happenings from the early 1960s particularly 'American'.[49] Rather, I would propose that the elision of a history of UK-based happenings from 'the history of art' is due not only to the early identification by Vostell, Becker, Szeemann and others of the twin origins of happenings in Kaprow and Fluxus, but also by the success of RoseLee Goldberg's multiple editions of her survey *Performance: From Futurism to the Present* first published in 1979 by Thames & Hudson.[50] That the same publisher of Henri's survey should promote a similar title merely four years after his would have only lessened *Total Art*'s chances of becoming a standard reference book.

More damaging still to the legacy of Henri's version of the history of happenings is his inclusion of multiple British, especially non-London-based artists and collectives, which would have hindered the book's appeal to an American readership. Whereas Goldberg's *Performance* traces live art back to the same origins as Henri's book – Futurism, Russian revolutionary art, Dada, Surrealism and the Bauhaus – she then jumps into the present with the chapter

'American and European Performance from c. 1933', where even the European exponents of performance art are seen from the vantage point of New York:

> Outside America, however, European and Japanese artists were developing an equally large and varied body of performances at the same time. By 1963, many of those, such as Robert Filliou, Ben Vautier, Daniel Spoerri, Ben Patterson, Joseph Beuys, Emmett Williams, Nam June Paik, Tomas Schmit, Wolf Vostell and Jean-Jacques Lebel *would have either visited or sent work* that indicated the radically different ideas being developed in Europe.[51]

Far from Goldberg to imagine that 'radically different ideas' would develop in Europe without much awareness, or care, of what was going in New York. The problem for Henri, however, was not his ignorance of what was happening in New York but on the contrary his awareness of the latest developments in live art on both sides of the Atlantic. The chapter 'Great Britain' in *Total Art* is difficult to read today, rife with now forgotten performance collectives in Edinburgh, Newcastle, Birmingham, Leeds, South Wales and, not least, Liverpool. Henri is clear about his provincial bias: as he writes, with few exceptions (these exceptions being Gallery One and the ICA), 'the London art world has tended to promote safe, easily saleable commodities...'; 'elsewhere in the country, ... it has been more possible for small, self-sustaining groups of artists to create multi-media works in a localised context'.[52] This bias blinded Henri to such exceptional performance sites in London as Better Books, where numerous groundbreaking performances took place, including a reading by Ginsberg in 1965 and environments by Latham, Bruce Lacey, Nuttall and others. But as Henri saw it, 'the provincial artist, at best, has a unique advantage: roots in a place, yet free of metropolitan commitment to current fashions, often more genuinely international in outlook'.[53]

In *Total Art* Henri declares that 'undoubtedly the most exciting mixed-media work in England today is being produced by young artists in Yorkshire'. Historically, though, he acknowledges another key site of early happenings in the UK, namely Edinburgh. If Liverpool could claim to have held the first such events in 1962, it was Edinburgh that attracted the UK's attention to the art form in 1963, when the second of an annual literature conference at Edinburgh University hosted a performance by Dewey featuring a nude woman.[54] The national outrage it provoked secured lasting recognition for happenings, albeit for the wrong reasons: 'Ever since then, the Great British Public has associated happenings with naked ladies', Henri humorously remarks in *Total Art*.[55] Still, in the friendly rivalry between Liverpool and Edinburgh, it was the former that acquired renown in the 1960s as a creative centre on par with, if not New York, then San Francisco, where music, poetry and art mixed with comparable intensity. (Edinburgh would soon gain the cultural upper hand in the second half of the 1960s and earl 1970s, mainly thanks to Henri's friend, the indefatigable artist and curator Richard Demarco.[56])

In the aftermath of the Beat poets, San Francisco played host to a vibrant and politicised performance art scene, with Anna Alprin's dance workshops and Ron Davis' San Francisco Mime Troupe, which performed Alfred Jarry's *Ubu King* in 1963.[57] It is no surprise, then, that thanks The Beatles, but also to its vibrant poetry scene, Liverpool was known around 1965 as the 'English San Francisco' while San Francisco itself was flattered with the moniker 'America's Liverpool'.[58] Whereas Los Angeles, New York and London dominated the cultural scenes in the US and UK respectively, San Francisco, 'the last refuge of the Bohemian remnant',[59] found an ideal twin cultural city in Liverpool.

If Goldberg's ignorance of happenings and performance in the UK, let alone in Liverpool and Edinburgh, would become an asset – allowing her to overlook previous work in the field, that is, Henri's, and credit herself with having written 'the first history of a medium with no real name'[60] – Henri's ability to combine histories of happenings in New York and Paris with provincial manifestations in Cologne, Liverpool, Edinburgh, Newcastle, Prague and Vienna would become a liability. By relinquishing the metropolitan-centred narrative favoured by Goldberg, and adopting a decentred, horizontal and internationalist approach, Henri was performing the very decentralising and democratising potential he claimed for performances and happenings. He was also, by the same token, writing himself out of modernist histories clinging to US-centred narratives. As he observes in *Total Art*: 'In England, though there have been influences from both American and Continental movements, there is, in the best work in the field, an urge to use environmental forms to by-pass the modern tradition of the isolated artist'.[61]

Where Goldberg holds onto the typically modernist role of critic and observer, claiming purchase over what counts as historically significant or not, Henri thrusts himself into the story he tells, endangering the seat of narrative power: 'The first happenings in England were done by a group of artists and poets in Liverpool in 1962, as a result of my reading an article by Allan Kaprow earlier that year. I had been making assemblages, and, as with Kaprow, happenings seemed a natural extension'.[62] One should not read Henri's repeated reference here to the acknowledged inventor of happenings as a wholesale acceptance of the normative history of performance with New York at its centre. Rather, the author of *Total Art* is resorting to Kaprow's 'brand name' to better introduce other, overlooked histories of performance, notably his own:

The 'events', as we called them, quickly became a popular form of entertainment: a mixture of poetry, rock'n'roll and assemblage. The early ones like *City* (1962), by Henri/John Gorman/Roger McGough, used a taped music track. Later events had live music by local 'Merseybeat' groups, for instance the Roadrunners and The Clayton Squares, as in *Nightblues*, 1963. The most popular of these were *Bomb* and *The Black and White Show*, held at the Cavern in 1964 and 1965, and written in collaboration with the poet Brian Patten, which were much more directly political in implication.[63]

Note the correlation between the more popular events (*Bomb* and *The Black and White Show*) with the more directly political. Here, I would suggest, is another reason for *Total Art*'s relative lack of success compared to that of *Performance Art*: the latter ends on the comforting note that performance art has now entered the mainstream ('Today, performance art has become a widely recognisable art form'[64]), while Henri's narrative ends with a section entitled *Art and Politics*, which itself concludes with the following paragraph accompanied by a drawing by Lebel of instructions on how to build a Molotov cocktail:

> Whatever the next developments in the visual arts may be, it seems certain that the museum, and the private collection of handmade masterpieces, will be increasingly irrelevant to a generation of artists who have returned to a far older tradition of social integration and interaction.[65]

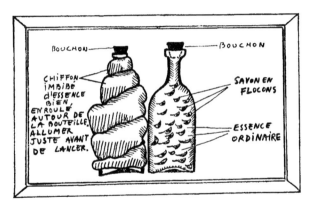

Jean-Jacques Lebel, *Do It Yourself*, 1969

The reference to Lebel is surprising, in light of Henri's tepid opinion of the French artist's 1966 book *Le Happening*, where the author sought to apply 'his theories of revolutionary social/artistic action and psycho-sexual liberation' to the new art form.[66] But Henri's commentary is also surprising for its characteristically post-May 1968 revolutionary language, which would have no doubt seemed antiquated by the beginning of the Thatcher era when Goldberg's upbeat conclusion that performance and entertainment are here to stay, as they always have, came out. Udo Kultermann's assertion, made in 1971, that the most important distinction of happenings are their refusal to be 'exploited for profit' was soon obsolescent, given the speed with which happenings turned into museum-friendly commodities.[67] Already by 1972, as Henri was writing about a thriving performance art scene across the UK in *Total Art*, he confessed that the year marked 'in some ways ... the end, rather than the beginning of something'.[68]

By 1975, a year after *Total Art* appeared, Liverpool could hardly merit the title of 'the centre of the universe'.[69] By the turn of the 1980s, if there was a total art at all, it would come from the US, and more precisely New York, to the detriment of all other 'centres'.

The transition from the 1960s to the 1970s was a difficult one for Henri, as it was for so many 1960s radicals. With overtly radical gestures like happenings gaining mainstream credentials, the line between the political and personal became harder to draw. Henri's 1971 *Autobiography* is a case in point: he conceded that the collection of poems 'was meant to be a political book, but the only way I could write it, eventually, was about me and my inability to do just that...'[70] The poetry/rock band The Liverpool Scene, which he fronted, met with popular, if not commercial success between 1967 and 1970, allowing the 'overweight, bearded Liverpool poet' to appear before hundreds of thousands of fans at rock concerts in the UK and, less successfully, the US.[71] But Henri's absence from Liverpool, and from his daily activities of painter, poet and teacher, made his return to his home city, after the band's breakup in 1970s, all the more difficult. Although he had correctly anticipated the growing importance of the entertainment industry, his life on the road with The Liverpool Scene had forced him to turn his back on what had made cultural life in Liverpool so distinctive: in the words of Michael Horovitz, its 'thriving club scene, a multi-racial late-night population and widespread unemployment'; or in Nuttall's, its combination of 'the old red-nose Lancashire comedian' and the 'crumbling grandeur of the nonconformist north'.[72] But Henri no longer wanted to communicate with the 'twenty people' who once regularly attended his readings and events; he wanted to address 'two million', while refuting the accusation that being popular means selling out.[73]

One could argue that it was not so much Henri but Liverpool itself that had changed. When he purchased his house in the late 1960s – thanks to the proceeds of *The Mersey Sound*[74] – the Liverpool of the early 1960s that had shaped his work, and that he had shaped in turn, was fast receding: the once active 'Bohemian community of painters and people all living around the Canning Street area'[75] disbanded at the turn of the 1970s, as some artists moved into what would become more acceptable addresses in Liverpool, or to other cities entirely. The signs were clear that the Swinging Sixties had passed for good.[76]

As Liverpool today aspires to recover its former glory as a cultural capital, it is tempting to celebrate uncritically the work of Henri and his 1960s peers, turning him, for example, into a preeminent 'love poet' or a bard of Liverpool. His house, voided of the presence of the artist, inevitably lends itself to becoming a shrine, his glass cabinets full of Victorian baubles now static remnants of a bygone era rather than vivid collages in progress.[77] Against this historical recuperation in the name of 'regeneration', possibly even more effectively than his paintings and poems, stands *Total Art*. Henri's attempt at transforming international and local histories of events and happenings into a total art was, and remains, a defiant act of cultural resistance. It is no coincidence that a visionary performance artist like Mike Kelley, as an art student at the University of Michigan in the mid 1970s, would find inspiration in *Total Art*, a book determined to decentralise and de-nationalise cultural production.[78] Today, thanks to the resurgence of interest in regional histories of performance art in the UK and elsewhere, Henri's survey is ready for a new readership. Yet the fact that the book had to wait close to four decades to be revisited would have been appreciated by Henri, a master at predicting his own demise and at mistrusting any form of authority.[79] The recurrence of Ubu Roi, the petulant king of Poland, in Henri's paintings, poems and performances is in this sense an apt self-portrait as anti-hero. Like others, Henri saw in Jarry's 1896 creation of Ubu both a cornerstone of the history of happenings and performance, and an ageless and ever-contemporary transhistorical figure.[80] But for Henri, Ubu would have played the additional role of caricature of himself as the king of an imaginary kingdom, that is, Liverpool. The 'diminutive, almost bewildered' figure, 'like a creature from outer space',[81] dared to depose the cultural hegemonies of the 1960s – London and New York – and transform 'home' into the capital of a creative empire, one where fiction and art are not the opposite of historical, social and political truth but its essential sidekicks.

Window Event for the launch of *Environments and Happenings*, Claude Gill Books, Oxford Street, London, 1974

1   Adrian Henri, 'Notes on Painting and Poetry', 117 in this volume (9 in typed version, Adrian Henri Archive, Estate of Adrian Henri, Liverpool).

2   Part of the 2014 Liverpool Biennial and curated by Catherine Marcangeli, 'Adrian Henri: Total Art' was held at the Exhibition Research Centre, Liverpool John Moores University, from 5 July to 26 October 2014.

3   On Liverpool's cultural ambitions and promotional strategy see Sara Selwood, 'Liverpool, Art City?', *Art in a City Revisited*, eds. Bryan Biggs and Julie Sheldon (Liverpool: Liverpool University Press/ the Bluecoat, 2009), 53–89.

4   *The Liverpool Scene*, ed. Edward Lucie-Smith (London: Rapp & Whiting, 1967), 15. For two, otherwise excellent, such 'eulogies', see *Summer of Love: Psychedelic Art, Social Crisis and Counterculture in the 1960s*, eds Christoph Grunenberg and Jonathan Harris (Liverpool: Liverpool University Press/Tate Liverpool, 2005) and *Centre of the Creative Universe: Liverpool and the Avant-Garde*, ed. Christoph Grunenberg and Robert Knifton (Liverpool: Liverpool University Press/Tate Liverpool, 2007).

5   From Adrian Henri, Part Four, *City* (London: Rapp and Whiting, 1969), non-paginated.

6   For comparison, see two attempts at decoding an artist's library after the owner's passing: Émeline Jaret, 'La bibliothèque matérielle de Philippe Thomas', in *Retour D'y Voir* 5 (2012): 195–209; and Magnus Schäfer, 'Unpacking a Library' in *Dealing With – Some Texts, Images, and Thoughts Related to American Fine Arts, Co.* (Berlin: Sternberg Press, 2011), 70–4.

7   Walter Benjamin, 'Unpacking my library' (1931), in *Illuminations*, ed. Hannah Arendt, trans. Harry Zorn (London: Pimlico, 1999), 68–9.

8   Allan Kaprow, *Assemblage, Environments & Happenings* (New York: Harry N. Abrams, 1966), 21.

9   Peter Selz, 'Notes on Funk', in *Funk*, exhibition catalogue (Berkeley: University Art Museum, University of California, 18 April–29 May 1967), 5.

10 Henri generally used 'events' as the Liverpool equivalent of 'happenings' (see Adrian Henri, 'Some Notes for "Bomb" Event', one-page typed document, 1964 [Adrian Henri Archive, Estate of Adrian Henri, Liverpool]). However, in what follows the distinction between happenings, events, performance and live art will be kept intentionally blurry, in deference to the lack of distinction of the art form itself.

11 Adrian Henri and Roger McGough, 'City Event: An Introduction', one-page, undated typed document (Adrian Henri Archive, Estate of Adrian Henri, Liverpool). Henri does acknowledge the connection between Liverpool performance-based poetry and Jazz – see the five-page, undated typed document, 5 (Adrian Henri Archive, Estate of Adrian Henri, Liverpool): 'In Liverpool ... the dominant accent on performance rather than the written word stems largely from visits some years ago by London jazz poets like Pete Brown and Spike Hawkins, who in their turn were obviously influenced by their US counterparts'.

12 As a counterpoint to this common claim, see Roger McGough's resistance to reducing the so-called Merseysound to performance in 'The Persistence of Wit: essay and interview by Stephen Wade', *Reading the Applause: reflections on performance poetry by various artists*, ed. Paul Munden and Stephen Wade (York: Talking Shop, 1999), 37–8.

13 Frank Milner's introduction to the exhibition catalogue *Adrian Henri: Paintings 1953–1998* (Liverpool: National Museums & Galleries on Merseyside/ The Bluecoat, 2000), 8.

14 Adrian Henri, 'An Oral Autobiography', in *The Liverpool Scene*, 45–6.

15 Glimpses of Rhyl's former glory can be found in Stephen Clarke's photographs of the town – see his *Ocean Beach Rhyl* published by Café Royal Books, 2014; and Emma Roberts' review of an exhibition of Clarke's photographs at Oriel Colwyn in *Periscope* no. 1 (2012): http://issuu.com/ mrdavedodd/docs/periscopei/11 (accessed 12 July 2014).

16 One of Henri's favourite Beat poets, Lawrence Ferlinghetti, is the author of arguably the best-known ode to the fair ground: *A Coney Island of the Mind* (San Francisco: City Lights, 1958). For an arresting cross-reading of psychoanalysis and the fairground, see *The Coney Island Amateur Psychoanalytic Society and its Circle*, ed. Zoe Beloff (New York: Christine Burgin, 2009).

17   John Willett, *Art in a City* (Liverpool: Liverpool University Press/the Bluecoat, 2007 [1967]), 184.

18   Ibid., 179.

19   Quoted in Phil Bowen, *A Gallery To Play To: the Story of The Mersey Poets* (Exeter: Stride, 1999), 7.

20   Paul Overy, 'House Painters', *Art and Artists*, August, 1967, 40.

21   Adrian Henri, 'Happenings by Michael Kirby', handwritten document, 1 (Adrian Henri Archive, Estate of Adrian Henri, Liverpool). Shortly after the publication of his *Happenings* book, Kirby guest edited a special issue of the *Tulane Drama Review*, vol. 10, no. 2 (Winter 1965), which Henri quotes in *Total Art*, 204 note 4.

22   *Happenings: An Illustrated Anthology*, ed. Michael Kirby (London: Sidgwick & Jackson, 1965), 11.

23   Ibid.

24   Richard Kostelanetz, *The Theatre of Mixed Means: an introduction to happenings, kinetic environments and other mixed-means performances* (London: Sir Isaac Pitman and Sons Ltd., 1970), xii-xiii.

25   Ibid., 27.

26   See Mildred L. Glimcher, *Happenings: New York, 1958–1963* (New York: The Monacelli Press, 2012), 72–3, 102–03, 118–19.

27   Barbara Haskell, *Blam: The Explosion of Pop, Minimalism, and Performance 1958–1964* (New York: Whitney Museum of American Art, 1984), 27, and also 37.

28   Kaprow, *Assemblage, Environments & Happenings*, 188.

29   *Adrian Henri: Selected and Unpublished Poems, 1965–2000*, ed. Catherine Marcangeli (Liverpool: Liverpool University Press, 2007), 12–4.

30   Henri, 'Some Notes for "Bomb" Event'.

31   Adrian Henri, 'Notes Towards a Definition of Performance Art', four-page undated [1975?] and unpaginated document (Adrian Henri Archive, Estate of Adrian Henri, Liverpool).

32   Edward Lucie-Smith compares Henri's so-called food paintings to Thiebaud in 'Adrian Henri: Poet–Painter Painter–Poet', *Art and Artists* vol. 3, no. 5 (August 1968): 38.

33   See David Hockney's designs for the production of *Ubu Roi* at the Royal Court Theatre in 1966 (Gene Baro, 'Hockney's Ubu', *Art and Artists*, May 1966, not paginated).

34   Jeff Nuttall, Bomb Culture (London: Paladin, 1968), 124. For an opposing view, whereby poetry in Liverpool owed little to The Beatles, see Andrew Wilson, 'A Poetics of Dissent: Notes on a Developing Counterculture in London in the Early Sixties', *Art & The 60s: This Was Tomorrow*, ed. Chris Stephens and Katharine Stout (London: Tate Publishing, 2004), 96.

35   Edward Lucie-Smith, 'Pop and the Mass Audience', *Studio International*, August 1966, 97.

36   Adrian Henri quoted in Edward Lucie-Smith, 'Adrian Henri: Poet–Painter Painter–Poet', 38.

37   Adrian Henri, untitled transcript of interview, c. 1967, 5 (Adrian Henri Archive, Estate of Adrian Henri, Liverpool). It is worth remarking that in a text from 1958, Kaprow suggested that merely aiming for a synthesis of the arts – as attempted by Wagner – was insufficient; only a 'different kind of art' that 'takes nature itself as model or point of departure' would achieve 'total art' ('Notes on the Creation of a Total Art', *Allan Kaprow: Essays on the Blurring of Art and Life*, expanded edition, ed. Jeff Kelley [Berkeley, Los Angeles, London: University of California Press, 2003], 10).

38   Adrian Henri, 'Notes on Painting and Poetry', 109 in this volume.

39   In 1965 Kaprow admitted to finding the term 'happening' a poor substitute for earlier expressions such as 'theatre piece', 'performance' or indeed 'total art', yet could not provide a viable alternative (Allan Kaprow, 'A Statement', in Kirby, *Happenings*, 47).

40   See also Vautier's related 'Total Art Match-Box' from 1968: http://www.moma.org/interactives/exhibitions/2011/fluxus_editions/works/total-art-matchbox-from-flux-year-box-2 (accessed 11 July 2014).

41   Frank Popper, *Art – Action and Participation* (London: Studio Vista, 1975), 24.

42   *Happenings: Fluxus, Pop Art, Nouveau Réalisme*, ed. Jürgen Becker and Wolf Vostell (Hamburg: Rowohlt, 1965), 36. For an almost Biblical narrative of the birth of the happening, see Glimcher, *Happenings: New York, 1958–1963*, 11:

'In early October 1959, thirty-two-year-old Allan Kaprow – an artist and professor – presented a performance piece entitled *18 Happenings in 6 Parts*. This unique conjunction of visual, aural, and physical events, performed for an intimate art world audience by his friends and colleagues, would change the course of art history. The new genre of artwork that evolved from this debut would become known as "Happenings"'.

43   See *Happenings & Fluxus*, exhibition catalogue, ed. Harald Szeemann and Hanns Sohm (Cologne: Cologne Kunstverein, 1970). The catalogue's preliminary section, entitled '*Vorchronologie und Parallelen*', nonetheless begins in 1951, and includes mentions of Gutai performances in Tokyo and Osaka from 1955–57.

44   See Harald Szeemann's introduction ('*Zur Ausstellung*') to the exhibition leaflet, a copy of which is in the Szeemann archives at Getty Research Institute, Los Angeles (Box 298, Folder 2). Szeemann's sustained interest in 'totalising' art projects is well documented, manifesting itself in such important exhibitions as '*Der Hang zum Gesamtkunstwerk*', which he curated at the Kunsthaus Zürich in 1983.

45   Kaprow, *Assemblage, Environments & Happenings*, 210.

46   Adrian Henri, *Total Art: Environments, Happenings and Performances* (London: Thames & Hudson, 1974), 12 (Schmidt), 170 (Vostell). In the same book, see the section entitled 'Further Reading', 208.

47   Judith F. Rodenbeck, *Radical Prototypes: Allan Kaprow and the Invention of Happenings* (Cambridge, Mass., and London: The MIT Press, 2011), 15.

48   Heike Roms and Rebecca Edwards, 'Towards a Prehistory of Live Art in the UK', *Contemporary Theatre Review*, vol. 22, no. 1 (2012): 18–9.

49   When Richard Kostelanetz writes that the 'new theatre is characteristically American in its frequent references to sub-artistic or "popular" culture', he is rehearsing the very American twentieth-century desire to identify home-grown (read: non-European) forms of art (Kostelanetz, *The Theatre of Mixed Means*, 28). This desire, articulated by such critics and artists as Clement Greenberg and Donald Judd, has more to do with nationalist sentiment than any art historical evidence, since 'frequent references to sub-artistic or "popular" culture' marked innumerable artistic manifestations outside the US during the 1960s, including Henri's in the UK.

50   The first edition of Goldberg's book was titled *Performance: Live Art 1909 to the Present*. The book has spawned numerous reprints, a sequel (*Performance: Live Art Since the 60s*), and led to Goldberg's initiative to found the performance art biennial, *Performa*, in New York in 2005. For better or worse, *Performance* has retained its status of 'seminal' textbook on the subject – see, for example, Jens Hoffmann and Joan Jonas, *Perform*, London: Thames & Hudson, 2005, 15.

51   RoseLee Goldberg, *Performance: Live Art Since the 60s* (London: Thames & Hudson, 1998), 85 – emphasis added.

52   Henri, *Total Art*, 111–12.

53   Adrian Henri, 'Coming from Somewhere', *The Guardian*, Thursday, 26 August, 1971, 9.

54   Robert Hewison, *Too Much: Art and Society in the Sixties 1960-1975* (London: Methuen, 1986), 104–5. Kaprow misdates the performance as having taken place in 1964 (*Assemblage, Environments & Happenings*, 283) – a mistake Henri repeats in *Total Art*, 86.

55   Henri, *Total Art*, 86.

56   On the origins of Richard Demarco's gallery in Edinburgh, see his 'A Rare Kind of Madness in Edinburgh', *Art and Artists*, January 1969, 24–7. Henri reviewed Demarco's important 1970 exhibition 'Strategy Get Arts' – see *Scottish International*, 12, November–December 1970, 43–4.

57   See *Looking for Mushrooms: Beat Poets, Hippies, Funk, Minimal Art – San Francisco 1955–1968*, exhibition catalogue (Cologne: Museum Ludwig/Walther König, 2009), 162–69.

58   See Jon Murden, 'Psychedelic Liverpool?', *Summer of Love*, 271; and, in the same volume, George McKay, 'Protest and counterculture in the 1960s', 54.

59   Karl Shapiro, quoted in Selz, 'Notes on Funk', 6.

60   Goldberg, *Performance*, 9.

61   Henri, *Total Art*, 111.

62   Ibid., 117.

63   Ibid.

64   Goldberg's final sentence of the first edition
     of *Performance Art* manages to make the
     very radicalism of performance art into a
     perfectly predictable historical reaction to
     limitation: '... it will always be a means to
     break through any limits or conventions
     imposed on art activity' (*Performance*
     [1979], 125). In the *World of Art* reprint of
     her book, Goldberg resorts to metaphor
     to drive her point home: '[Performance]
     history is like a series of waves; it has
     come and gone, sometimes seeming to be
     rather obscure or dormant while different
     issues have been the focus of the art world'
     (*Performance* [1988], 210).

65   Henri, *Total Art*, 185.

66   Although he calls Lebel's book *Le
     Happening* (Paris: Denoël, 1966) 'useful' in
     Total Art, Henri shows little enthusiasm
     for it in an undated handwritten four-page
     book review (3, Adrian Henri Archive,
     Estate of Adrian Henri, Liverpool).

67   Udo Kultermann, *Art – Events and
     Happenings*, trans. John William Gabriel,
     (London: Matthew Miller Dunbar, 1971), 80.

68   Henri, 'Notes Towards a Definition of
     Performance Art', not paginated (Adrian
     Henri Archive, Estate of Adrian Henri
     Liverpool).

69   'Liverpool is no longer, as Ginsberg ten
     years ago said it was, the centre of the
     Universe, but [Henri's and McGough's]
     poetry survives and flourishes'
     (*Conversations*, ed. Mike Davies,
     [Birmingham: The Flat Earth Press, 1975],
     i, ii).

70   Ibid., 6.

71   See the interview with Adrian Henri,
     (Adrian Henri Archive, Estate of Adrian
     Henri, Liverpool): 'At that time [in 1970]
     too all kinds of things began to happen
     to me in a personal way – the last remains
     of my family all died in that year. That
     was a traumatic experience...' On Henri's
     return to Liverpool after the US tour of
     The Liverpool Scene, see Mike Evans,
     'The Liverpool Scene', notes for the CD
     *The Amazing Adventures of... The Liverpool
     Scene* (London: Cherry Red Records, 2009).

72   Robert Hewison, *Too Much*, 97; Nuttall,
     Bomb Culture, 123.

73   *Conversations*, 6–7.

74   Communication with Catherine Marcangeli,
     24 July 2014.

75   Adrian Henri, untitled transcript of
     undated interview (1, Adrian Henri Archive,
     Estate of Adrian Henri, Liverpool).

76   Darren Pih, 'Liverpool's Left Bank',
     Centre of the Creative Universe, 118, 126.

77   Milner, 'Introduction', *Adrian Henri:
     Paintings 1953–1998*, 11.

78   See *Mike Kelley: Minor Histories*, ed.
     John C. Welchman (Cambridge, Mass.
     and London: The MIT Press, 2004), 69.

79   See 'Adrian Henri's Last Will and
     Testament', *Underdog* no. 5, 1964,
     non-paginated.

80   See Kostelanetz, *The Theatre of Mixed
     Means*, 23–4; and Goldberg, *Performance*
     [1979], 9–10.

81   Michael Kustow, 'Adrian Henri: Notations
     for an Audio-Visual Album', exhibition
     leaflet, *Adrian Henri: Paintings and
     Drawings* (London: The Institute of
     Contemporary Arts, 1968), non-paginated.

'A noisy kind of abandoned thing': Adrian Henri and Music

Bryan Biggs

In the context of total art, Adrian Henri holds a singular position. This creative polymath embraced visual art, poetry, performance, music and critical writing. Very few artists manage to successfully combine such a breadth of practice, reputations resting instead on the privileging of a single art form. Artists with parallel careers in different disciplines struggle to be taken seriously in more than one of them, especially so where music is concerned – Laurie Anderson being a notable exception, scoring a number two UK hit record in 1981 with *O Superman* without compromising her avant-garde credentials as a performance artist.

At the level of musical celebrity there is good reason for this non-transference of genius into other disciplines: the paintings and drawings of Bob Dylan, Joni Mitchell, Miles Davis or Paul McCartney, for instance, pale next to their monumental musical achievements, generally being regarded as hobbyist activities that do little to enhance their artistic reputations. The art world gives short shrift to 'interlopers' from outside, witness the indifference shown to music mavericks KLF's K Foundation 'worst artist' award presented to Turner Prizewinner Rachael Whiteread, or its burning of a million pounds.[1] The advice given to Don Van Vliet by his art dealer in the early 1980s was to focus completely on his painting if he wanted to be taken seriously in the contemporary art world, his genuinely innovative musical persona, Captain Beefheart, effectively being retired as a result.

The visual arts – and the art school in particular – have however provided a fertile environment for individuals to try their hand at different things, pursuing visual and performing arts, especially music, in tandem, the distinctive look and sound of British pop music being the most celebrated outcome of this process. While the likes of John Lennon, Pete Townshend, David Bowie and Bryan Ferry, whose Roxy Music was conceived as a 'work of art',[2] achieved success in the music industry, a successful visual artist like Christian Marclay has created art from the materiality of pop itself through his performances, recordings, assemblages and 're-mixing' of record sleeves, musical instruments and films; or Turner Prize-winner Martin Creed regularly performing and releasing records, following figures like John Hyatt, who combined painting (one of which was featured on the cover of the 1984 *British Art Show* catalogue) with fronting Leeds post-punk trio The Three Johns.

Henri was not a trained musician, yet music informs much of his work and is a thread that weaves its way through his practice, particularly in the 1960s and 1970s. Art school-trained, he saw himself first and foremost as a painter, though it was poetry that brought him success. However, for a brief period in the late 1960s it was as a gigging musician that he gained a degree of national recognition fronting poetry rock band The Liverpool Scene, who despite their records' lack of commercial success, were enormously popular on the live music circuit, supporting the likes of Led Zeppelin [Fig. 87] and Sly & the Family Stone, and performing at the 1969 Isle of Wight festival, and even having their own regional TV show.[3]

Henri's multi-disciplinarity was not achieved alone, but through collaboration, and in music this is most evident. His work with The Liverpool Scene occupies a large part of this chapter, but music was also significant as inspiration and subject for poems and to a lesser degree paintings, as well as in his live and recorded poetry readings and multi-media performances. There is musical rhythm too in his poems, even when not accompanied by the guitar of long-standing collaborator Andy Roberts. Henri followed Robert Frost's advice to 'Take care of the sounds, and the sense will take care of itself',[4] and believed that 'the "formal" or perhaps better "musical" values are what make poetry poetry'.[5]

A trawl through what survives of Henri's record collection reflects an eclectic breadth of taste and interests that characterises his entire artistic output. Classical, jazz, folk and rock albums sit side-by-side, genres whose references litter his poetry, particularly in his earliest published volumes. In *Who?*, the poet wonders with whom he can listen to the French *chansonnier* Georges Brassens, who else can sing along to Shostakovich, and who to buy the next Miles Davis record for. Amongst Henri's heroes listed in *Me*, musicians and composers feature prominently: John Coltrane, Charles Mingus, Debussy, Bach, Charlie Parker, Bessie Smith, Berg, Bartók, Shostakovich, Roland Kirk, Manfred Mann, Miles Davis, Stravinsky, Thelonious Monk, Cannonball Adderley, Mick Jagger and all of The Beatles. 'The Entry of Christ into Liverpool' [Fig. 38] progresses to the rhythm of a marching band, the fife and drum of an Orange Lodge parade, while 'April Message' repeats the Liverpool football club terrace chant 'Ee-ay-addio', and 'Song of Affluence' or 'I Wouldn't Leave My Little 8-Roomed House for You' is based on a 1905 music hall song, *I wouldn't leave my little wooden hut for you*. It's as if Henri is providing in these poems a condensed history of music, both serious and vernacular, in the first half of the twentieth century, from classical to jazz, blues to soul, and the giddy, contemporary 1960s pop world, to which he, together with Roger McGough and Brian Patten, provided a pop poetry equivalent, as well as participating himself as the decade's music progressed in a heavier direction, pop groups turning into rock bands.

Classical music references are woven into poems of romantic and domestic reverie such as 'The Blazing Hat, Part Two' where 'beautiful girls with Renaissance faces played Hindemith records', and 'Love Story' – 'listening to Bruckner in the sunlit bathroom' – which, when performed with Roberts' hypnotic acoustic guitar accompaniment, represents one of Henri's most successful poetry/music combinations. The elegiac tone of 'Without You' is accentuated in its evocation of Mahler's final composition, with its expression of the redemptive power of love: 'Without you Mahler's 8th would be performed by street musicians in derelict houses'.

A fan of New Orleans jazz, Henri caught the homegrown variety live when still a teenager, watching Freddy Randall, 'Britain's No. 1 Dixieland Band', perform in 1950 at the Pavilion Theatre in Rhyl. Art school in Newcastle provided further opportunities to immerse himself in jazz, and Henri joined the King's College Jazz Band, which judging from the washboard he is playing in a photo of the band, incorporated skiffle, the transition from 'trad' to rock'n'roll for many young musicians in the latter part of the decade. Back in Rhyl in the early 1960s, he joined the Bee Jazz Club, as did future musical collaborator Mike Evans.

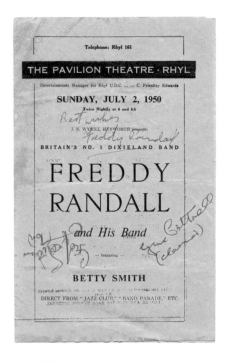

Programme for Freddy Randall and His Band, The Pavillion Theatre, Rhyl, 2 July 1950

Adrian Henri playing washboard with the King's College Jazz Band, c. 1954

With his tastes moving from trad to bebop, to the latest modern jazz emanating from New York, Henri soaked up the music of Davis, Adderley, Monk, Coltrane and Mingus, paying homage to the latter in one of his most celebrated poems, 'Tonight at Noon', its title lifted from a 1957 Mingus recording (released in 1965). Comprising surreally construed paradoxes inspired by the tune's title, the poem's musical references ironically are not jazz: 'Folksongs are being sung by real folk', 'Poets get their poems in the Top 20'. Interestingly, the cover illustration to Mingus' *Tonight at Noon* LP on Atlantic Records by the label's art director, Marvin Israel, combines surreal and abstract imagery, photography and expressive painting, which would have appealed to Henri, particularly the design's (perhaps unconscious) nod to Jasper Johns' flag paintings. In 'Adrian Henri's Last Will and Testament' he leaves his 'Charlie Mingus records to all Liverpool poets under 23 who are also blues singers and failed sociology students'.

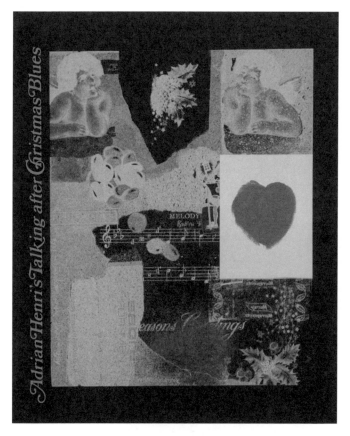

Adrian Henri, *Talking After Christmas Blues*, limited edition book, with music score by Wallace Southam (London: Turret Books, 1969)

The blues idiom also inspired several poems, the 'talking blues' form that Woody Guthrie and later Bob Dylan popularised providing a framework for Adrian Henri's 'Talking After Christmas Blues', while 'Car Crash Blues' or 'Old Adrian Henri's Interminable Talking Surrealist Blues' adopts the standard 12 bar structure, one employed later in The Liverpool Scene's parody of late 1960s British blues bands, 'I've got those Fleetwood Mac Chicken Shack John Mayall can't fail Blues'. Henri further acknowledged Black American music in his lyrics, referencing popular soul singers: 'No more blues by Otis Redding' in 'Nightsong', and Wilson Picket's 'In the Midnight Hour', adopted as the title for a poem that sees 'The Beatles singing "We Can Work it Out" with James Ensor at the harmonium/Rita Hayworth in a nightclub singing "Amade Mia"'.

Given the dominance of pop over all other musical genres in the 1960s, it is not surprising that Henri absorbed the latest hits and pop fads, just as television and advertising provided equally rich material for his poems and paintings. He had worked during the previous decade at Rhyl's seaside fairground so would have been exposed to its soundtrack:

Frankie Laine Guy Mitchell
loud through the electric nightrides
(from 'Autobiography')

Deafened by music from all sides
   Johnny, remember ...
   She's a square ...
   Baby, I don't care ...
(from 'Fairground Poem')

The raucous rock'n'roll hits from American legends like Duane Eddy, Dion and the Belmonts and Johnny and the Hurricanes, pumped out at full volume as the dodgems dodged and the waltzer waltzed, would inspire The Liverpool Scene's fictional group, Bobby and the Helmets, whose doomed leader Henri would become for several thrilling minutes during the band's popular finale *The Woo Woo*. [Fig. 84]

With Liverpool producing the most influential pop group of the era, local beat music was bound to inform Henri's work: 'Merseybeat ... got me into liking other kinds of music apart from jazz,' including modern classical composers Shostakovich and Stravinsky,[6] as well as The Beatles and other bands performing in the early 1960s at the Cavern, for which Henri had a membership card, and where he staged his own happenings involving beat musicians (and later, in 1968, a residency with The Liverpool Scene). The Penguin Modern Poetry volume *The Mersey Sound* featuring Henri, McGough and Patten, was launched at the Cavern in 1967 to the accompaniment of local rhythm & blues band, The Almost Blues.

It was here and at other Merseybeat venues that Henri encountered the teenage girls he would christen, after William Blake, 'The Daughters of Albion' – wearing 'lavender at The Cavern or pink at The Sink', trying out the latest dance craze at the drop of a handbag, to pop tunes supplied by

> Beautiful boys with bright red guitars
> in the spaces between the stars
>
> Reelin' an' a-rockin'
> Wishin' an' a-hopin'
> Kissin' an' a-prayin'
> Lovin' an' a-layin'[7]

This celebration of live beat music and appropriation of lyrics from pop hits – Chuck Berry's 'Reelin' And Rockin'' (1959) and Hal David and Burt Bacharach's 'Wishin' and Hopin'', a hit for Dusty Springfield in 1964 – complemented by the more risqué "a-layin'", is echoed in Allen Ginsberg's eulogy to the 'Liverpool minstrels of Cavern' in 'Who To Be Kind To' and The Beatles themselves in 'Portland Coliseum', as well as in other poems from the mid-Sixties.[8] During Ginsberg's visit to Liverpool in 1965 he famously described the city as 'at the present moment the centre of the consciousness of the human universe. They're resurrecting the human form divine there – all those beautiful youths with long, golden archangelic hair'.[9] Henri recalls taking Ginsberg to the Cavern and other venues to taste Merseybeat first hand, drummers from local beat groups jamming with the Beat legend, who played Tibetan rhythms on a set of finger cymbals.[10] The heavily amplified music in a sweaty Liverpool club environment was a new experience for the American, who would grow closer to the world of electric rock music, particularly during the psychedelic years in California and his later musical collaborations in New York.

References to The Beatles and the 'Swinging Sixties' abound in Henri's poems: a policeman partially blinded by a jelly baby thrown at a passing pop singer; an inquest into the death of Paul McCartney (in 'The New "Our Times"'); McCartney again, met 'in a suburban garden wearing a moustache drawn by Marcel Duchamp' ('Hello Adrian'); fantasising in 'I want To Paint' of painting 'The Beatles composing a new National Anthem', 50 nudes of Marianne Faithfull,

✳

Rapp & Carroll limited

will be

____ pleased
____ tolerant
____ amused
____ disgraced
____ ecstatic
____ poorer
____ grateful
____ surprised

if you attend their party at

The Cavern, Liverpool

to celebrate the publication of

the liverpool scene

Friday	*R.S.V.P./A.S.A.P.*
March 3	128/134 Baker Street
2.30 - 5.30 pm	London W 1

Invitation card to the launch of Edward Lucie-Smith's *The Liverpool Scene*, at The Cavern, 1967

'Charlie Mingus playing the Mike Evans songbook', Jagger doing TV commercials for travel-sickness pills, Coltrane with a band of angels playing solo; listening, in 'Summer Poem Without Words', to the 'B' side of the latest Dusty Springfield record. For Henri, 'Love is when you're feeling Top of the Pops/Love is what happens when the music stops' ('Love Is…'). In 'Love Poem', 'ANY RECORD IN THE TOP 20 ANYTIME IS OUR TUNE,' 'The Beatles sing lullabys for our never-to-happen children,' 'Bartók has orchestrated the noise of the tulips in Piccadilly Gardens for us,' and Charlie 'Parker blows another chorus of Loverman for us'.

Music then, be it classical or jazz, soul or pop, provided Henri with multiple devices for his poetry: as lyrical content and rhythmic structure, and as cultural reference points, both historical and contemporary. Music elements were a point of access for an audience for whom the traditional barriers between high art and popular culture were breaking down.[11] The mass communication media of radio and television and the expanding circuit for live music, combined with the seismic shift in Western cultural spearheaded by The Beatles, ensured that pop music was the *lingua franca* and the means through which new ideas of the 'young generation' percolated. We shall see later how the performance of music live also played an important function in Henri's embrace of total art.

Surprisingly perhaps, there are only occasional musical references in Henri's paintings – far fewer than in his poetry, and less evident than in the contemporary Pop paintings of Peter Blake or fellow Liverpool painter Sam Walsh, two artists whose portraits of The Beatles and others reflected how pop stars' iconic status was being achieved with the help of cheap, mass produced photographic images circulated through magazines and record sleeves, cards and badges. Henri was not a portraitist, but like Blake used paint and collage in compositions that pay homage to his musical heroes. In *24 Collages, No. 4 Clayton Squares Painting* (1964) [Fig. 36], over a painted Yves Klein blue ground he pastes publicity photos of Merseybeat combo The Clayton Squares, including future Liverpool Scene member Mike Evans, together with the group's autographs and roughly sketched purple hearts (presumably any drug reference here is unintended). 'I love Cliff' is scrawled on the surface of another collage/painting, *Small Fairground Image I* (1961) [Fig. 2].

In the major painted work *The Entry of Christ into Liverpool in 1964* (1962–64) [Fig. 37], amongst the crowd of Henri's heroes and friends are The Beatles and, leading the procession, an imposing Mingus attired in traditional Chinese dragon costume, painted from a photo of the jazz legend used on the cover of his 1959 *Mingus Dynasty* EP. Standing to the left of Mingus is British poet Pete Brown who, like Henri, integrated music into his live readings and went on to front his own poetry rock bands. Amongst the crowd's flags and banners, a placard enigmatically declares 'The Disc Box', an apparent reference to a local record shop run by Henri's friend, Orrie Hafkin.[12] Completed in 1964, the painting anticipates the composition of the most iconic record cover of that decade, that of *Sgt. Pepper's Lonely Hearts Club Band* (1967), another collage of Liverpool heroes largely selected by The Beatles, designed by Peter Blake and Jann Haworth, and based on an idea by Paul McCartney, though it is not known if the Beatle had seen Henri's painting. Over 30 years later, Henri reworked the format of *The Entry of Christ* in another large-scale painting, *The Day of the Dead, Hope Street* (1998), whose dancing and guitar-strumming *calaveras*, modelled on Mexican artist José Guadalupe Posada's popular prints, continue the carnivalesque dance in Liverpool's streets.

A key text on the origins of the avant-garde in the twentieth century, Roger Shattuck's *The Banquet Years: The Arts in France, 1885–1918* (1955),[13] may have provided Henri with a template for total art. This study of *fin de siècle* Paris with its cast of characters from four different creative disciplines – *naïf* painter Henri Rousseau, composer Erik Satie, poet Guillaume Apollinaire and absurdist playwright Alfred Jarry – exerted an influence on Henri, not just through his adoption of the persona of Jarry's monstrous creation, Père Ubu. The book pointed to the possibility of interdisciplinarity, which Henri took a stage further by coalescing all these artforms into a single practice – the artist as painter-poet-performer-musician, a composite Jarry/Apollinaire/Satie/Rousseau. Focussing on the centre of the avant-garde's postwar shift to New York, Calvin Tomkins adopted Shattuck's approach in *The Bride and the Bachelors* (1962),[14] an examination of the interdisciplinary practices of composer John Cage, mixed media painter Robert Rauschenberg, 'machine sculptor' Jean Tinguely and grandfather of the avant-garde, Marcel Duchamp. By the time this book was published in Britain, Henri had already staged several 'events', arguably the first performance art in the UK, which put the idea of the multimedia experiment into practice, and music was again an essential ingredient.

Heavily influenced by American artist Allan Kaprow, these 'mixed-media experiments incorporating the three Ps – poetry, painting and pop'[15] were significantly different to New York happenings, including in their use of music. Technical requirements, for instance, that Henri lists in his notes for the *City* event (1962) [Figs. 4–8] held in Hope Hall, the basement of a former Methodist church on Hope Street (now The Everyman Theatre), include two tape recorders with sound effects of the city, a gramophone and a portable radio tuned to pop station Radio Luxembourg for most of the action. *Daffodil Story – an experiment in Communication* (1963) starts with a 45 rpm record, *Along Came Jones* by US doo wop/novelty rhythm & blues band The Coasters, includes The Beatles' 'I want to hold your hand', and ends with dancing to the overture to Jarry's play *Ubu Roi*. There was an assortment of sonic and musical elements in these events and, unlike the preference in US happenings to use experimental/improvised music or modern jazz – by now appreciated as a serious modern art form – Henri chose to incorporate the hits of the day, further positioning his events within a pop culture rather than high art context when he introduced live beat groups into the mix. While Henri describes an improvisatory 'jazz attitude' at the core of these early events, 'what musicians call "head-arrangements" (i.e. not written out but largely pre-determined)',[16] he did not use jazz musicians, and in fact argued against the use of improvisation in his happenings, carefully scripting everything instead: 'I use music as the limiting factor'.[17] According to Mike Evans, the sixth of these events, *Nightblues* (1963) featuring The Roadrunners, was a 'breakthrough', significantly moving the music/verbal elements of the performance from poetry and jazz to poetry and rock/rhythm & blues.[18] *Bomb* event (1964) followed at the Cavern, involving Evans' group The Clayton Squares, who participated in further events with Henri in 1965: *Spring* at the Bluecoat and, together with The Excelles and local DJs Billy Butler and Bob Wooler, *Black and White Show* at the Cavern.

An outcome of these events was to demonstrate the potential of combining spoken word with live music in a structured way that both brought greater concentration on the poem itself and allowed space to create complementary sonic ambience. The nature of Henri's and the other Mersey poets' work lent itself to being performed rather than just read, and from these early experiments he refined his live readings, initially with guitar accompaniment and eventually performing with a full band. Poetry and live music was not new. In London, poetry and jazz were being performed together in concerts organised by Jeremy Robson featuring Adrian Mitchell, Laurie Lee, Dannie Abse and Christopher Logue, who also recorded an EP, *Red Bird*, with The Tony Kinsey Quintet.[19] Michael Horovitz's New Departures visited British towns and cities between 1960 and 1965, the first touring jazz and poetry group in the country, coming in Henri's words 'to evangelise the north,' including Liverpool.[20] A concert, *Blues for the Hitch-hiking Dead*, at the Crane Theatre in 1961 featured Horovitz, Pete Brown and Mark (Spike) Hawkins with The Art Reid Quartet. Henri was disdainful of poets improvising with jazz: 'Some of the English poetry-and-jazz people make exaggerated claims about this and some poets I know are constantly re-writing their work'.[21] Pete Brown describes the poetry he was then writing 'in loosely musical forms like chase choruses. Theoretically it was pretentious but what saved it was the humour and a certain Britishness'.[22]

If these experiments were unsuccessful artistically, the efforts of Brown and Hawkins – 'hitch-hiking evangelists of the London poetry/jazz circuit'[23] – were however instrumental, working with 'local unknowns', in getting the Liverpool live poetry scene going in the early 1960s, with readings at Streate's coffee house on Mount Pleasant hosted by Dubliner Johnny Byrne who, with Hawkins, relocated to the city. This was the archetypal 'cellar club', candlelit and with whitewashed walls, duffle coats and modern jazz. It 'was to poetry what the Cavern was to rock'n'roll'.[24] Musical accompaniment was a regular feature of these poetry readings and, at Sampson & Barlow's basement beneath the Peppermint Lounge on London Road and other venues, was increasingly played by electric bands, notably The Almost Blues and The Clayton Squares. In contrast to New Departures' proselytising, it was pop and rhythm & blues, not jazz, that offered a way forward for the emergent pop poetry, a path more in tune with the local Merseybeat. The critic Edward Lucie-Smith noted the similarities between a poetry event and a pop gig: 'the audience is hardly conscious that there *is* a distinction'.[25] The poetry circuit attracted the same young people who followed The Beatles and other groups at the Cavern, rather than a traditional literary or exclusively 'arty' crowd. According to Mike Evans, Ringo Starr and George Harrison turned up in the audience at one Hope Hall poetry reading.[26] From this scene The Scaffold emerged, a poetry and satire trio formed by McGough, John Gorman and Paul McCartney's brother Mike McGear, who secured a record deal with Parlophone, going on to score a Top Ten hit with their third single *Thank U Very Much* in November 1967 and a Number One, *Lily the Pink*, a year later. Pop poetry clearly had wider commercial appeal beyond the confines of Liverpool's cellar clubs. As McGough observed, 'the kids didn't look on it as Poetry with a capital 'P', they looked on it as modern entertainment, part of the pop movement'.[27]

Adrian Henri and Andy Roberts waiting to go on stage, Granada Road Show, 1969

University law student Andy Roberts started to accompany Henri on acoustic guitar in 1966, following sessions he'd done with McGough that included an early version of 'Summer with Monika'.[28] Before arriving in Liverpool that year, the guitarist had experienced poetry performed with music at The Arts Theatre, Cambridge, the Michael Garrick Trio backing Laurie Lee, Dannie Abse, Thomas Blackburn and Jeremy Robson, a recipe that he, like Henri, felt didn't work for the poets.[29] Henri and Roberts therefore set out to see if they could create a different combination to this uneasy fusion, and over the next few months fine-tuned a collaborative approach, one which worked because Roberts' 'poem specific' accompaniments were 'at one with the mood and content of the poems'.[30] Early in 1967, the regular weekly sessions of poetry, folk song, humour and happenings at The Everyman Theatre were complemented by Liverpool's first 'Poetry and Blues' concert featuring what Henri described as 'collaborations' between himself, McGough, Roberts and The Almost Blues, a move towards a more consciously integrated music and poetry night out that – reflecting Henri and McGough's obsession with Batman comics – would culminate in the 'famous Bat Rave featuring all concerned in a fitting homage to the Caped Crusaders'.[31]

Lucie-Smith's interest in the poetry scene around Henri, McGough and Patten resulted in the publication in 1967 of *The Liverpool Scene* anthology,[32] which was launched at the ICA, London, and led to a BBC2 *Look of the Week* TV appearance and a gig at London's underground hangout, UFO. CBS issued an accompanying LP *The Incredible New Liverpool Scene*, featuring McGough and Henri reading. Recorded over a couple of hours in studios in London's Denmark Street, the LP did not include Patten, the third of 'The Trinity' of poets in *The Mersey Sound* volume, but did feature Roberts' guitar accompaniment. Radio London pirate DJ John Peel picked up on it, playing it on his *Perfumed Garden* programme, thus beginning a relationship with Henri and Roberts that would see him, nominally at least, produce the first album of their poetry/rock group The Liverpool Scene.

The Liverpool Scene, ed. Edward Lucie-Smith (London: Donald Carroll, 1967)

By mid-1967, events such as The Everyman Theatre poetry and blues concert and a 'Liverpool Seen' 'Halloween Drop Out' at the Sink club together with Roberts' University band The Trip had convinced Henri and Roberts – now joined by 'failed sociology student' Mike Evans, poet and saxophonist with The Clayton Squares, and another 'second wave' Merseybeat musician, singer and guitarist Mike Hart from The Roadrunners – that a poetry/music show would work. Following Roberts' suggestion that all they needed to become a bona fide rock band was a bassist and drummer, Percy Jones (from The Trip) on bass and Brian Dodson (from local bands Rogues Gallery and The Earthlings) on drums completed the line up,[33] some of the band living communally at 64 Canning Street, an address immortalised in one of Roberts' Liverpool Scene songs, '64'. The band's name, The Liverpool Scene, was what audiences referred to them as, dubbed from the Lucie-Smith book title, and was formally adopted for a *Love Night* event at The Everyman Theatre. [Fig. 30] Establishing a residency at Hardman Street bar, O'Connor's,[34] the transition from poetry/acoustic music to a full rock band was complete, and The Liverpool Scene entered the 'progressive' rock and folk scene, gigging and recording over the next three years until folding in 1970.

A reason perhaps for Henri wanting to move into pop music territory was his envy of what pop stars could do, the greater freedom he felt they had compared to poets:

> Because of the whole pop aura that surrounds their work they could allow themselves obscure or very personal images or sounds *and their public will accept it*. Whereas we always have to worry about the problem of communicating: what *can't* you allow yourself to say. I think this is a marvellous situation, for them. I think Dylan falls into the obvious trap this freedom opens, sometimes: The Beatles always seem to avoid it. Because no matter how interested in Oriental music or post-Stockhausen techniques they are they always seem aware of their responsibility as entertainers.[35]

This sense of responsibility to one's audience, of needing to entertain, is a trait of Liverpool culture that Henri rightly detects in The Beatles, and is party behind Liverpool poet Paul Farley's assertion that the city does not embrace 'dissonance'.[36] As Henri's early performance events and poetry readings with music had shown, it *was* possible to incorporate serious themes, complex ideas and unfamiliar juxtapositions into work that had popular appeal, and a touring rock group provided another context that would potentially make his work accessible to an even wider audience.

The Liverpool Scene shared a breadth of musical backgrounds that included jazz, beat, folk and blues, all of which were effectively deployed to create evocative settings for the poems of Henri, Evans and a non-band member, the Liverpool painter Maurice Cockrill ('Happy Burial Blues'). Working within a conventional rock format, their live performances were however unlike the regular late-1960s progressive or hard rock fare. 'We do a noisy kind of abandoned thing', Henri declared, stressing that they only came together as a band for the last half hour of their set, the rest of the time being devoted to individual performances of poetry and songs.[37] Lyrically, the band was amongst the most innovative on the underground music circuit, producing songs that were both reflective and topical, combining intelligence with humour. Much of this came through the choice of Henri's poems – many already published – but also Evans' verse and solo songs in a contemporary folk vein by Roberts and Hart, whose acerbic, Dylan-inflected songs were 'inescapably great – howls of socio-political rage that really hit home'.[38]

Roberts reflects that 'we did it all – rock, jazz, folk, funny, sad, sexy, thought-provoking. No one else even scratched the surface of what we were after. We wanted to be the complete package, the undeniably great night out in the pub with something for everybody. We loved it'. Essentially 'a straightforward heavy drinking bunch of blokes, with very few other drugs',[39] they journeyed the length and breadth of Britain. *Their* reality was not so much the acid-fuelled path to spiritual enlightenment eulogised by contemporary psychedelic bands like Mighty

Baby or Quintessence, or the cerebral meanderings of The Third Ear band, as the tedious grind of the M1 motorway (which then didn't even reach London), grotty changing rooms and the dispiriting transport cafes and service stations immortalised in Roy Harper's 'Watford Gap'.[40] While they could create sublime moments in their music, for instance where Roberts' delicate, raga-infused guitar or Jones' inventive bass interacted with Henri's aching lyrics, and audiences would be exposed to Henri's eclectic range of influences – Apollinaire, Jarry, Baudelaire, James Ensor, Alfred Bester, the Beats – The Liverpool Scene did not share the esoteric preoccupations of London's hip cognoscenti with its embrace of Eastern philosophies, alternative lifestyles and mind-altering substances.

Educated and intensely literary, the band was also resolutely proletarian, reflecting a northern sensibility through songs of everyday urban life – often infused with Scouse surrealism – singing humorously for instance about being on the dole ('that was the day the NAB was fab'[41]) long before punk and with none of its nihilism. Though long-haired and wearing the trappings of hippie couture, they equally drew on dockers' attire, Henri's donkey jacket, knotted scarf and peaked cap contrasting with the Frank Zappa-looking Dodson's woolly hat and ankle-length leather coat.[42] Merseyside might have produced *the* pop group who came to embody the 'Swinging Sixties', but things swung differently in Liverpool, a predominantly working class city with nothing like the wealth, nor the hip entrepreneurs and concentration of media and fashion industries that drove London's preeminence as international pop capital. While Liverpool's poetry scene perhaps provided 'the local alternative to psychedelia ... the local vehicle for any "spirit of '67" that might have existed',[43] there was still a sense – as elsewhere in the northern provinces – of a city not fully recovered from the shattering effects of the War World Two and, in contrast to the capital's financial buoyancy, a port in irreversible economic decline. Liverpool's bomb sites and crumbling tenements provided a gritty, photogenic backdrop for The Liverpool Scene's publicity shots, but this was the lived reality for many of the city's inhabitants.[44]

Unlike the Jimi Hendrix- and Cream-influenced rock histrionics of the era, the tedious drum solos, instrumental jams and cosmic, self-indulgent lyrics, The Liverpool Scene's concerts offered a more down-to-earth experience (but were not without the customary freak-out finale), consciously designed with the audience in mind. This was largely a result of Henri's experience refining his poems: 'a Liverpool audience was (a) great influence as they would only accept what was lively. Doing poetry readings forced him to re-write some of his poems, improving them with simplification as he sought to achieve a degree of closeness with the audience'.[45] This propensity to entertain chimed with fellow art-influenced combo, the Bonzo Dog Doo-Dah Band (their name a corruption of Dada). Both bands shared a tongue-in-cheek sophistication in their knowing musical referencing and the way they sought to mix up high culture with the vernacular. They were irreverent towards the contemporary pop and rock world and some of its more

Liverpool Scene promotional
photograph, c. 1969

earnest phenomena like the 'British blues boom', the Bonzos asking 'Can blue
men sing the whites?', while Henri lampooned leading blues merchants in 'I've
Got Those Fleetwood Mac Chicken Shack John Mayall can't fail Blues', which
concluded with him imitating a 'jobsworth' caretaker of a small venue clearing up
at the end of a long night, moaning that 'I fought in the War for the likes of you'.[46]
No doubt such a scene would be accompanied by Henri and the rest of the band
hustling to get paid after the gig, the 'bread on the night' of their second LP's title.

A feature in the influential underground fortnightly *International Times (IT)*
reveals a London perspective on The Liverpool Scene, written in characteristic
countercultural language:

> They booze and screw and talk like ordinary layabouts ... It's poetry about
> commonplaces which is inspiring because of its naturalness. Away from the
> sherry party and the perverseness of the London literary world. London is
> rich, pretentious, hostile.
>
> 'But although things need changing, life is worth living. They enjoy it even
> when living on milk and cheese the day before they collect their National
> Assistance. Living and the practice of their art are equally important.
> Being a musician or a poet is the same thing as being a clerk or a labourer.
> It's something that you can do, so you do it. Art is robbed of its snobbery
> and mystery. Culture is made popular. At last English poetry becomes a
> democratic art form. But they don't say they're important. That's up to the
> pundit creeps.[47]

London, crucible in the late 1960s of new forms of artistic expression such
as experimental theatre, 'head' music, expanded cinema, and the sort of art form
crossovers that Henri pioneered at the start of the decade, produced surprisingly
few bands that combined the same mix of poetry, music, theatricality and politics
as The Liverpool Scene. Experimentation on the capital's music scene resided
elsewhere: the sensory multi-media environment of underground clubs UFO and

Middle Earth produced the likes of Pink Floyd and The Soft Machine, but their early experiments with light shows and improvisation soon gave way to a more strictly musical focus. Pink Floyd's lyrical ingenuity and looseness largely evaporated after Syd Barrett left, while through Robert Wyatt's Jarry-inspired 'pataphysical' innovations, The Soft Machine (named, with the author's permission, after a William Burroughs novel) maintained something of their early surrealism, but this disappeared in the drive towards jazz-rock conformity. The Bonzos, arguably the closest equivalent to The Liverpool Scene in terms of their live shows, took their warped trad jazz into ever more absurd territory, driven by frontman Viv Stanshall's increasing eccentricity and Neil Innes' musical and songwriting craftsmanship.

Liverpool Scene concert advert, Melody Maker, November 2, 1968

There were other groups performing poetry with music: The Barrow Poets, formed in the late 1950s – originally mixing existing texts, from Shakespeare to Kerouac, with a classical and traditional music repertoire including Mozart, Purcell and folk, and eventually integrating their own poetry and releasing records over a 40-year career (they last performed at the turn of the new millennium) – and the short-lived Occasional Word Ensemble, whose awkward blend of Scaffold-inspired poetry, sketches and acoustic blues can be heard on their sole 1969 album on John Peel's Dandelion label (which also released Mike Hart's post-Liverpool Scene solo records). But it was Henri's old pal Pete Brown who sought to integrate his brand of British beat poetry into an electric band context, developing his First Poetry Band into increasingly more rock-oriented ensembles, The Battered Ornaments and then Piblokto! This move from the poetry and jazz combination of Horovitz's New Departures to a hard rock format was accelerated by the success of Brown's songwriting collaboration with Jack Bruce, bassist of Cream, their 1966 hit 'Wrapping Paper' being the first result of this partnership.[48] Unlike The Liverpool Scene though, where Henri mainly read his poems over a backdrop of musical embellishments, Brown was very much a lead singer in his bands, his lyrics sung rather than recited as poems (by his own admission, his range though was limited).

The Liverpool Scene's progress as a popular live band started when John Peel invited them to play on some of his college gigs alongside favourites Tyrannosaurus Rex [Fig. 79], Roy Harper, Principal Edwards Magic Circus and Davy Graham, as well as performing regularly on Peel's BBC radio show. The band quickly built up a following on the 'progressive' rock circuit of universities and clubs like Mothers in Birmingham [Fig. 82], Van Dikes in Plymouth,

London's Roundhouse and The Farx in Southall and Potter's Bar, playing alongside many of the darlings of the alternative music scene like Jethro Tull, Fairport Convention and Colosseum. They also played more unusual venues: the Caius College Cambridge all night May Ball, a raucous affair according to Roberts,[49] where the bill also included a rare appearance from reclusive singer songwriter Nick Drake;[50] and London's premier jazz venue, Ronnie Scott's, where – while multi-instrumentalist Roland Kirk played the main stage – The Liverpool Scene performed upstairs, receiving somewhat faint praise from jazz purist Miles Kington:

> pop poet ... Henri has been sniped at by every literary critic worth his salt for exposing himself on the printed pages, so it is only fair to say that in his own context – reciting throwaway poetry in small intimate surroundings – he is quite effective. Certainly, his off-hand but carefully worked out delivery in front of his group is more satisfying than the pretentious mating of jazz and poetry ever managed to be.[51]

Mike Hart left the Liverpool Scene after the first LP and drummer Brian Dodson was later replaced by Pete Clarke, the band becoming, in Mike Evans' opinion, increasingly proficient but 'inevitably, less anarchic and spontaneous, which undoubtedly was part of our original charm'.[52] Their popularity did not wane however, and by May 1969 they were at their peak with the release of second album *Bread on the Night*, followed by a tour that took in the Bath Festival of Blues, the stage apparently 'groaning' under Henri. Here the bill also included Fleetwood Mac, Chicken Shack, Savoy Brown and John Mayall – the four blues bands parodied in 'I've Got Those Fleetwood Mac Chicken Shack John Mayall can't fail Blues'. In the festival's official programme, blues label Blue Horizon repaid the 'compliment' with a full-page advert announcing 'We've got those Fleetwood

The Liverpool Scene, *Bread on the Night*, RCA, 1969

Mac Chicken Shack Champion Jack Dupree Blues'.[53] The next day, The Liverpool Scene's 'Pop Proms' gig with Led Zeppelin and Blodwyn Pig at London's Royal Albert Hall [Fig. 87] ended with all three bands jamming together on rock'n'roll standard *Long Tall Sally* after Henri had 'done [his] bit with the collapsing trousers and the gold lame underpants'.[54] The band then played to an estimated 150,000 at 'Britain's Woodstock', the second Isle of Wight Festival of Music, headlined by Bob Dylan and featuring a folk-oriented programme that included Tom Paxton, The Pentangle, The Band and Richie Havens. As Brian Hinton recalled in *Message To Love*, his chronicle of the Isle of Wight festivals:

" **WE'VE GOT THOSE FLEETWOOD MAC CHICKEN SHACK CHAMPION JACK DUPREE BLUES** "

BLUE HORIZON

Manufactured and distributed by CBS Records

Advert in the official programme for the Bath Festival of Blues, 1969

> First on were The Liverpool Scene with their mixture of pop and poetry. Overweight, bearded Liverpool poet Adrian Henri
> bounded about the stage with remarkable energy. 'Let's see if we can wake up Bob Dylan from here', he yelled. And he went into a number (*The Woo Woo*) about an American rock'n'roll group who died when a soda fountain exploded in New York, drowning 200 people in soda ice-cream.[55]

Pathé News footage screened nationally at cinemas shows an anarchic performance with Henri cavorting about the stage and Evans lying on his back honking his sax. While whipping up the audience in this way, the band proved they could equally achieve silence from the crowd, as during Henri's poignant 'Winter Poem', accompanied by Jones' haunting bass.

The *IT* feature suggested that 'Sneerers call the Liverpool Scene the Adrian Henri Show. He's the link man, but the group emerge as individuals'.[56] Though all band members made significant contributions, Henri was still however very much the group's figurehead, a 'jovial penguin' similar to other physically large front men in the music business of the time – Bob 'The Bear' Hite of American blues boogie band Canned Heat, British rhythm & blues legend Graham Bond, Henri's friend the Liverpool-born surrealism expert, jazz singer and entertainer George Melly, even Demis Roussos (then lead singer in Greek psychedelic pop band Aphrodite's Child) – part of a tradition stretching back to blues shouters Howlin' Wolf and Big Mama Thornton. Whilst all of these could sing with force, Henri's vocal, as opposed to his reading, abilities were limited, a pre-punk yeller, heard to best effect in *The Woo Woo*.[57] However, as surviving films of gigs, live recordings and reviews of those shows demonstrate, he was certainly effective: 'Exhorting,

swearing, blaspheming, shouting and raving, Adrian roused the hitherto peaceful audience into a near-anarchistic frenzy'.[58]

The vocal abandon of 1950s rock'n'roll novelty throwback *The Woo Woo* was also heard in another popular live song, *Baby,* where Henri's singing becomes increasingly demented as the number turns into a rant against the English Conservative MP Enoch Powell, whose notorious 1968 'Rivers of Blood' speech was attacked for stirring up racial hatred. With its audience participation refrain of 'We don't want you, Enoch', the song was in a similar vein to The Edgar Broughton Band's anthem *Out, Demons Out!* and reflective of the alignment of underground music with the radical politics of the period, seen most expressly in bands like The (Social) Deviants in the UK and The MC5 in the US.[59] This was the period of student protests and 'third world' liberation struggles, and Evans and Roberts recall participating in a 'Revolution' poetry and music event at The Everyman Theatre.[60] Henri's political commitment can be traced back much earlier: he'd been on five anti-nuclear Aldermaston CND marches, was a member of the Committee of 100 and had been arrested twice on its demonstrations. Appointing anarchists Bakunin and Kropotkin as executors of his will,[61] politics were always important for him, and political events featured in his poems and in several of The Liverpool Scene songs and sketches such as Henri's *Bomb Commercials,* Evans' *Amazing Adventures of Che Guevara,* and others opposing the war in Vietnam, racism and nuclear proliferation – 'serious themes,' notes Evans, 'but pitched with an instinctively populist edge, a balancing act at which Adrian was becoming increasingly adept'.[62]

A favourite Liverpool Scene theme that lent itself to juxtaposing poetry with experimental soundscapes was science fiction, performed to particularly good effect in Evans' 'We'll All Be Spacemen Before We Die' and Henri's 'Universes'.

Opposite page: The Liverpool Scene (Adrian Henri and Mike Evans on stage), Isle of Wight Festival, 31 August 1969

Left: The Liverpool Scene, Granada Television Recording Studios, 1969

The 22-minute word and sound collage 'Made in U.S.A.', a diary of the band's 1969 American tour and centred on Henri's and Evan's alternating poems, which was recorded for the band's final LP, is bookended with references to that year's moon landing and also includes a nod to Stanley Kubrick's groundbreaking film from the previous year, *2001: A Space Odyssey*. Enhanced in the studio by the addition of accomplished UK jazz musicians,[63] the track is arguably The Liverpool Scene's finest achievement in bringing poetry and music together. Its combination of different musical styles, sound effects and words, as in earlier songs such as 'The Entry of Christ Into Liverpool', echoes Henri's collage approach employed across his practice. Such numbers demonstrate the greater depth in the performance of his poetry that The Liverpool Scene allowed him, from the jaunty ska rhythm of 'Love Is' and accelerating pace of the Batman TV theme tune adapted for 'Batpoem', to the atmospheric evocations of 'Winter Poem' and 'Love Story'.

Between 1968 and 1970, The Liverpool Scene produced three LPs for RCA Victor: *Amazing Adventures of…*, with a gatefold sleeve showing the band and a crowd of friends assembled outside O'Connor's, and on the inside cover a photo of them posed at Liverpool's pre-regeneration Albert Dock; *Bread on the Night*, ironically subtitled '9 Great Hits'; and *St. Adrian Co., Broadway and 3rd*, comprising a side recorded live at Warwick University and a side devoted to the aforementioned 'Made in U.S.A' [Fig. 64]. Whilst some of the material has dated, much of it has stood the test of time, and together these albums represent a substantial body of work by a band that was unique in its melding together of fine musicianship and poetic force.[64]

It was a recipe however that failed to translate to America, the continent that was a significant musical inspiration for the band, and culturally more broadly for Henri with his connection to Beat writing, to New York painting and happenings. Mike Evans describes Liverpool's 'cultural trappings' as always being American: 'In many ways Liverpool has been the New Orleans of English rock … the scene of a unique and localised musical movement that subsequently spread nationally and worldwide' (although most musicians had to leave the city to make it)'.[65] Especially from the 1950s onwards, influenced by transatlantic connections, most notably the 'Cunard Yanks', Liverpool's fascination with American popular culture made it arguably the most 'American' of British cities. A reciprocal embrace in America of all things Liverpudlian however was limited to Beatlemania,

Newspaper advertisement, The Liverpool Scene supporting Sly and the Family Stone, Kent State University, Ohio, 1969

and by the time of the second 'British invasion' of groups towards the end of the decade, there was no guarantee of success for bands visiting from these shores, and The Liverpool Scene's US tour in 1969 was, according to Roberts, a gruelling and revelatory three months, an 'absolute disaster'.[66] They supported The Who, The Kinks, Joe Cocker, Led Zeppelin, and at Kent State University, Ohio, in front of an audience of 17,000, Sly and the Family Stone, one of America's hottest live acts following their sensational appearance at Woodstock earlier in the year. Roberts' verdict on the tour was philosophical:

> We suddenly came up against the utter reality of it. With a British audience, given this poetry and a band that were never rehearsed, we got away with it through being so different and (through) our verve and irreverence. None of which worked in America.[67]

Their poetic emphasis was undoubtedly a drawback in the US.[68] A year earlier however Frank Kermode, reviewing the *Incredible Liverpool Scene* LP in *The New York Review of Books*, had praised Henri and Roberts' collaboration,[69] and a preview of a gig in Chicago claimed that The Liverpool Scene were remaking the earlier Beat efforts of Ginsberg and Lawrence Ferlinghetti in the US to fuse poetry and music with bongos, 'only better'.[70] New York's underground paper *East Village Other* was also sympathetic, recording an interview with Henri and Roberts at St. Adrian and Company, the aptly named local bar that provided the title for The Liverpool Scene's third LP. The interviewer had 'an interest in people like Adrian who had gone into other art forms to get their message across', citing Beat poet Ed Sanders' foray into rock'n'roll with the shambolic, proto punk, agit-prop New York group The Fugs. Henri, like Sanders, used his awareness of twentieth-century art and music movements to poke fun at them, and had an ambition to 'discover "how far poetry can be pushed and still remain poetry." His search takes him into every medium, and anyone attuned to the present will enjoy the trip'.[71]

After the band split up, Henri continued for a while in the rock business as a member of the loosely organised satirical outfit Grimms along with Roberts and members of The Scaffold, The Bonzos and other British music stalwarts. Leaving the band in 1973, Henri's musical career was effectively over, though music continued to be a significant part of his live readings, accompanied by Roberts, and he later teamed up with Liverpool rhythm & blues unit, The Lawnmower, whose leader Alan Peters, former member of The Almost Blues, had worked with Henri during the poet's earlier musical sorties.

It is undeniable that Henri's embrace of music as a means to enhance and, literally, amplify his words was facilitated by being in Liverpool during this vibrant musical period, when the city 'seemed like the capital of the world: for those of us living there then, it was a heady though disconcerting experience'.[72] The cosmopolitanism of what became more familiarly known as Toxteth, particularly the area he lived in where Liverpool 8 met Liverpool 1, with its febrile bohemia of poets, musicians, academics, prostitutes and layabouts, its art school, performance venues, iconic cathedrals, black clubs and characterful pubs like Ye Cracke and the Philharmonic, provided a catalyst and subject matter for Henri's work. From this environment's raw materials came key elements used in performances – in events, readings and music gigs – that broke down the old distinctions between art forms and between high and low culture. The sounds, voices and songs of Liverpool 8 provided a sonic backdrop for his poetry, just as the musical rhythms of his poems have produced a richly textured soundtrack for this district. From the poignancy of Henri's words interacting with Roberts' guitar to The Liverpool Scene's 'noisy kind of abandoned thing', it is a sound that continues to reverberate far beyond.

Poetry reading with music, c. 1968
(Mike Evans, Andy Roberts, Adrian Henri, Mike Hart)

1   Since Jimmy Cauty and Bill Drummond staged these events in 1994, the latter has found some accommodation in the art world, with an increasing number of projects involving exhibitions, events and publications in collaboration with galleries in the UK and internationally, including an ambitious world tour that began in Birmingham in 2014, where it will end in 2025.

2   See Michael Bracewell, *Re-make/Re-model: Art, Pop, Fashion and the Making of Roxy Music, 1953-1972* (Faber and Faber: London, 2007).

3   Granada TV commissioned the band for four half-hour shows, *The Liverpool Scene look at…*, broadcast in February 1969. Recorded live in the studio, edited together with filmed location sequences, the programme's themes were the seaside, love, Liverpool, and the future.

4   Adrian Henri, 'Notes on Painting and Poetry' in *Tonight at Noon* (London: Rapp and Whiting, 1968), 67 – and 112 in this volume. Frost's dictum, written in a letter to his friend Louis Untermeyer, is an inversion of the Duchess' advice to Alice, 'Take care of the sense, and the sounds will take care of themselves', in Lewis Carroll's *Alice's Adventures in Wonderland* (1865).

5   Henri, 'Notes on Painting and Poetry', 68 (Rapp and Whiting) and 113 in this volume.

6   Interview in Kingston Grammar School magazine (1970).

7   From 'Mrs Albion You've Got a Lovely Daughter', a nod to Herman's Hermits' 1965 hit 'Mrs Brown you've got a lovely daughter' – for the complete poem, see 12 in this volume.

8   In 'Middle Of A Long Poem On "These Shores"' (1966), Ginsberg quotes from Frank & Nancy Sinatra's hit 'These Boots Were Made For Walking' and references The Beatles' 'Michel' (sic) and 'Dancing to Can't Get No Satisfaction'.

9   Quoted in *The Liverpool Scene*, ed. Edward Lucie-Smith, (London: Donald Carroll, 1967), 15.

10   Ibid., 17.

11   This blurring of boundaries is reflected in *A Policy for the Arts: The First Steps*, Jennie Lee's 1965 White Paper, produced in her role as the Labour Government's first Arts Minister. It argued for, amongst other things, the need to bridge the gap between high art and popular culture.

12   Disc Box had two shops, in Lodge Lane, Liverpool and another in Birkenhead, where Mike Evans worked briefly after dropping out of college in 1963 (email to the author from Evans, May 2014).

13   Published in the UK in 1959 by Faber and Faber, London.

14   Published in the UK in 1965 as *Ahead of the Game: Four Versions of Avant-garde* (London: Weidenfeld & Nicolson).

15   Mike Evans, sleeve notes to the CD compilation *The Amazing Adventures of … The Liverpool Scene* (London: Cherry Red Records, 2009).

16   From the introduction to *City* event by Henri and Roger McGough.

17   Henri, 'Notes on Painting and Poetry', 68 (Rapp and Whiting) and 113 in this volume.

18   Evans, *The Amazing Adventures of …*

19   *Red Bird*, Parlophone, WEP 8765 (1959).

20   Folder 13, Adrian Henri Archive, Estate of Adrian Henri. Such concerts continued, and Henri in fact participated in a two-day poetry conference in Nottingham, 'Poetry '66' – an initiative of the Trent Book Shop in response to the 'International Poetry Incarnation' at the Albert Hall, London the previous year – that included 'A Concert of Poetry and Jazz with New Departures and Leading Poets', though it is not clear that Henri was in that line up (see http://clok.uclan.ac.uk/6457/1/CUSPNeate.pdf [accessed July 2014]).

21   Henri, 'Notes on Painting and Poetry', 68 (Rapp and Whiting) and 112 in this volume.

22   Pete Brown interviewed by John Platt for sleeve notes to Brown's 'best of' double LP, *Before Singing Lessons 1969-77*, Decal LIK D7 (1986).

23   Mike Evans, *The English Rock Explosion*, unpublished manuscript (1976).

24   Roger McGough, *Said and Done* (London: Arrow Books, 2005), 149.

25   *The Liverpool Scene*, 7.

26   Evans, in ibid.

27   Quoted in *The Liverpool Scene*, 78.

28   Performance at the Bluecoat, Liverpool.

29   Roberts interviewed by Colin Hall in an article on The Liverpool Scene, *Shindig* 19 (November–December 2010): 28.

30   Ibid.

31   Henri's notes on a flyer for The Everyman

Theatre concert, 7 February 1967. He also describes his preference for working with Beat groups since the early 1960s 'through working together on "Events" (Liverpool for happenings) and preferring this to the then fashionable poetry-and-jazz'.

32   An earlier study of the beat scene and the interaction between music, poetry and art, *Beat in Liverpool*, ed. Jürgen Seuss, Gerold Dommermuth, Hans Maier (Frankfurth: Europäische Verlagsanstalt, 1965) also features Henri and The Clayton Squares and includes excellent photographs by Seuss that evoke the period.

33   Dodson was replaced after the first LP by Pete Clarke, who in turn was replaced for the band's final weeks by Frank Garrett.

34   Liverpool singer songwriter Jimmy Campbell was unimpressed by the 'in crowd' at O'Connor's, as expressed in his 'Adrian Henri's Party Night' (from the LP *Son of Anastasia*, Fontana, 1969).

35   Henri, 'Notes on Painting and Poetry', 79 (Rapp and Whiting) and 121 in this volume.

36   Paul Farley in conversation with Mark Haddon, *The Guardian*, 3 April 2010, 12–13: 'Liverpool isn't about dissonance. It's hung up on tunes. Believe me, I've tried dissonance. But I keep coming back to the music'.

37   Henri in 'The Superstars in their own words' (1970).

38   Roberts, *Shindig*, 29.

39   Ibid., 31.

40   Harper's scathing description of Watford Gap service station from 1977, where you could enjoy a 'plate of grease and a load of crap'.

41   From Evans' 'The day we danced at the dole'. The NAB was the National Assistance Board.

42   Henri varied his stage costumes: 'bulbously resplendent in two hundred yards of white drill cotton loosely fashioned into a unique style of cricket trouser, plus assorted badges, thongs and beards' (Brian Harrison, review of The Liverpool Scene gig at Nottingham Technical College, *Iota* magazine, March 1969, 10).

43   Evans, *The English Rock Explosion*.

44   Henri has argued that the non-metropolitan origins of much of the UK's experimental arts scene – 'Pop' poetry and 'concrete' poetry in the 1960s and performance art

in the late 1960s/early 70s – in places like Liverpool, Cardiff, Yorkshire, Newcastle and Edinburgh stemmed from these places' localised contexts, existing contacts with international avant-garde movements, and distance from London fashions. (*Environments and Happenings*, [London: Thames & Hudson, 1974], 111-12.)

45   From an article, '"Liverpool Scene" Magnificent', including an interview with Henri, in an unidentified Portsmouth College of Art and Design publication, relating to the band's performance at Portsmouth's Sunday Night Blues Club, 1969.

46   The track 'Can blue men sing the whites?' appeared on second LP, *The Doughnut in Granny's Greenhouse* (1968), by which time the band had shortened its name to The Bonzo Dog Band. The Liverpool Scene track with this monologue by Henri is on *Bread on the Night* (1969).

47   Roger Mortimore, *IT* 31 (17-30 May 1968).

48   Both Bruce and Ginger Baker of Cream had performed earlier in jazz and poetry events.

49   Email from Andy Roberts to the author, April 2014.

50   Nick Drake was scheduled to come on at 3.30am with the 'orchestral work of Robert Kirby', after Bobo & Babs providing 'thrills and laughs on the trampoline'! (Caius College May Ball programme, 10 June 1969.)

51   Miles Kington, 'A month of Kirk', review in *The Times*, 7 March 1969. Kington did another, slightly more complimentary review of the gig in *Punch*, 12 March 1969, 393: 'the whole thing works extremely well on its own modest scale. (Jazz and poetry was always much less modest and always fell flat on its face)'.

52   Evans, *The Amazing Adventures of ...*

53   The programme for the festival (part of the Bath Festival), which was headlined by Led Zeppelin, has an incongruous foreword by Sir Michael Tippett: 'Get off to a good start and don't stop until you have to'. Predominantly an outlet for British blues performers, Blue Horizon also had American blues artists like Champion Jack Dupree on its roster.

54   From Henri's sleeve notes to the *Recollections* LP (1972). The underpants are on display at the Museum of Liverpool.

55   Brian Hinton, *Message to Love: Isle of Wight*

Festival, 1968, 1969, 1970, Sanctuary (1996). Bobby and the Helmets were an imaginary band, the creation of Adrian Henri and The Liverpool Scene. The great undiscovered band was supposed to have drowned in a soda fountain, cutting short a stellar career. When The Liverpool Scene toured with Led Zeppelin in 1969, Robert Plant and Jimmy Page went along with the joke and started wearing Bobby and the Helmets t-shirts, leaving all their fans wondering about the mysterious band.

56   Mortimore, *IT* 31 (17-30 May 1968).

57   A member of the Musicians Union, Henri's membership card describes him as 'Vocalist, Lyricist'.

58   Hugh Nolan, 'Pop Proms – a riotous start', review of Pop Proms gig in *Disc and Music Echo*, 5 July 1969, 6.

59   Though in reality such bands' sloganeering was not tied to any effective political agenda.

60   Emails from Mike Evans and Andy Roberts to the author, April 2014.

61   In Henri's poem 'Adrian Henri's Last Will and Testament'.

62   Evans, *The Amazing Adventures of ...*

63   Jazz musicians Ian Carr and Karl Jenkins from jazz rock luminaries Nucleus and Malcolm Griffiths, and Ian Whiteman from Mighty Baby. An early proponent of the fretless bass, Percy Jones went on to join UK jazz fusion band Brand X, which also included Phil Collins.

64   Two singles were also released as well as three further LPs after the band split, comprising two 'best of' collections in 1972 (*Recollections* on Charisma, and *Liverpool Scene Featuring Adrian Henri & Andy Roberts* on Polydor) and previously unreleased material (*Heirloon* on RCA in 1970). The most recent release is the double CD compilation *The Amazing Adventures of...* on Cherry Red Records (2009).

65   Evans, *The English Rock Explosion*.

66   See Roberts' website, http://www.andyrobertsmusic.com/

67   Ibid.

68   As suggested in American underground magazine *Kiss*, vol. 1, no. 28, 1969.

69   *The New York Review of Books*, 23 May 1968.

70   *Chicago Tribune* preview of a concert by The Who, The Kinks and The Liverpool Scene at the city's Kinetic Playground, 1969.

71   Allan Katzman, 'Poor Paranoids', in the *East Village Other*, October 1969, 11 and 15. Started in 1963–64 by Sanders and fellow Beat poet Tuli Kupferberg and Ken Weaver, the Fugs' anarchic poetry/rock was an American precursor to The Liverpool Scene, albeit less musically proficient and with a much rawer and more confrontational anti-establishment stance.

72   Henri, *Environments and Happenings*, 116.

Timeline

1932
- Born in Birkenhead

1938
- Family moves to Rhyl, North Wales

1951–55
- King's College, Newcastle-upon-Tyne, University of Durham Department of Fine Art; lecturers include Lawrence Gowing, Roger de Grey, Victor Pasmore, Richard Hamilton

1956
- Teacher, Catholic College for Boys, Preston
- Meets Joyce Wilson
- Returns to Liverpool
- Summer job at Rhyl fairground (returns over subsequent summers)

1957
- Scenic artist, Liverpool Playhouse
- Marries Joyce Wilson (divorces 1974)

1957-58
- Teacher, schools in Manchester and Liverpool

1958
- In Rhyl meets Mike Evans (later member of The Clayton Squares and The Liverpool Scene)
- First exhibition, *Liverpool Academy Open*, Walker Art Gallery, Liverpool

1959
- Exhibition, *Five Painters* (Adrian Henri, Henry Graham, Alan Wood, Don McKinlay, Anthony Collinge), Bluecoat Gallery, Liverpool
- *Spring Exhibition*, Cartwright Hall, Bradford

1961
- Meets Roger McGough, Brian Patten, Spike Hawkins and Pete Brown
- Poetry Readings, Liverpool
- Part-time Lecturer, Manchester College of Art (Foundation Course)
- *John Moores Liverpool Exhibition 3*, Walker Art Gallery, Liverpool

1962
- Begins painting *The Entry of Christ into Liverpool*
- *City* event with Roger McGough and John Gorman for the Merseyside Arts Festival, Hope Hall, Liverpool
- *Death of a Bird in the City* event with Roger McGough and John Gorman for the Merseyside Arts Festival, Hope Hall, Liverpool
- *The Machine* event with Roger McGough and John Gorman for the Merseyside Arts Festival, Hope Hall, Liverpool
- Exhibition, *Adrian Henri and Sam Walsh*, Portal Gallery, London and Hope Hall, Liverpool

1963
- *Paintings, Daffodils, Milkbottles, Hats* event with Roger McGough and John Gorman for the Merseyside Arts Festival, Hope Hall, Liverpool
- *Man* event with Roger McGough and John Gorman for the Merseyside Arts Festival, Hope Hall, Liverpool
- *Nightblues* event with Brian Patten and The Roadrunners, Hope Hall, Liverpool
- Exhibition, *Pop Art*, Midland Group, Nottingham
- Exhibition, *New Images from the North*, Hope Hall, Liverpool (organised by Adrian Henri for the Merseyside Arts Festival)

1964
- Lecturer, Liverpool College of Art (Foundation Course, until 1967)
- *Bomb* event with The Clayton Squares, The Cavern, Liverpool
- *Night: a poem with and without words* event with Brian Patten, Hope Hall, Liverpool
- *Open Exhibition*, The Ulster Museum, Belfast
- Arts Council of Northern Ireland prize (£200)

1965
- *Spring* event with The Clayton Squares, Bluecoat Chambers, Liverpool
- *Black and White Show* event with The Clayton Squares, The Excelles, Billy Butler and Bob Wooler, The Cavern, Liverpool
- Exhibition, *Industry and the Artist*, Walker Art Gallery, Liverpool
- *John Moores Liverpool Exhibition 5*, Walker Art Gallery, Liverpool (jury includes Clement Greenberg)

1966
- Meets Edward Lucie-Smith, who is researching *The Liverpool Scene*
- Film for 'New Release' BBC Television by Liz Kustow

1967
- *The Mersey Sound*, collection of poems with

Roger McGough and Brian Patten (Penguin Modern Poets no. 10)
- *The Liverpool Scene* edited by Edward Lucie-Smith and published by Rapp & Carroll
- *Love Night* event, The Everyman Theatre, Liverpool
- LP *The Incredible New Liverpool Scene*, with Roger McGough and Andy Roberts
- Poetry/Rock Group The Liverpool Scene formed with Andy Roberts, Mike Evans, Percy Jones, Brian Dobson and Mike Hart
- *John Moores Liverpool Exhibition 6*, Walker Art Gallery, Liverpool
- Exhibition, *Art in a City*, ICA, London

1968
- Resigns from Liverpool College of Art
- Meets Susan Sterne
- Stays with John and Ann Willett in Le Thil, Normandy; returns most summers until 1998
- *Tonight at Noon*, published by Rapp & Whiting
- *I Wonder*, play on Guillaume Apollinaire written with Mike Kustow, ICA, London
- *Revolution, Revolution, Revolution*, performance by The Liverpool Scene with Adrian Mitchell and Christopher Logue, The Everyman Theatre, Liverpool
- LP *Amazing Adventures of...* The Liverpool Scene
- Exhibition, ICA, London (solo show)
- Exhibition, New Institute Gallery, Birmingham (solo show)
- Exhibition, Midland Group, Nottingham (solo show)
- Exhibition, *Poetry Posters*, Brighton Festival and Fulham Gallery, London
- Exhibition, *Biennale della Giovane Pittura*, Milan
- Exhibition, *Aargh! The Spirit of the Comics*, ICA, London

1969
- Meets Nell Dunn and begins writing *I want*
- North West Arts Association Writers on Tour
- *City* published by Rapp & Whiting
- The Liverpool Scene, performances at Bath and Isle of Wight Festivals
- The Liverpool Scene, tour of USA and UK with Led Zeppelin
- LP *Bread on the Night*, The Liverpool Scene, released by RCA
- *Adrian Henri's Talking after Christmas Blues*, with music by Wallace Southam, published by Turret Books

- *The Liverpool Scene*, Granada Television
- Exhibition, Leeds Art Centre (solo show)

1970
- Death of parents and grandparents; ordered to rest for six months due to ill health
- The Liverpool Scene, *St Adrian Co., Broadway & 3rd*, released by RCA (cover design by Henri)
- Break up of The Liverpool Scene
- *Poems for Wales and Six Landscapes for Susan*, published by Arc Press
- *Autobiography*, Poems Nos. 1–15 commissioned for the City of London Festival
- Poetry International Festival, Rotterdam (returns to give poetry readings until 1996)
- *Cultural Bingo*, Performance/event/environment, The Blackie, Great Georges Project, Liverpool (game devised by Bill Harpe)
- The Liverpool Scene, *Heirloon*, released by RCA
- *Henri and Friends*, tour of Norway
- *Grub*, children's workshop with Susan Sterne, ICA, London

1971
- Visiting Lecturer, Bradford and Wolverhampton Polytechnics
- Meets Frances Hambidge
- *Autobiography*, published by Jonathan Cape
- North West Arts Association Writers on Tour
- Grimms, roadshow formed with Roger McGough, John Gorman, Mike McGear, Neil Innes, Vivian Stanshall, Zoot Money, Mike Giles and others (Keith Moon for one night); tour to Ireland, Scotland, Norway and South West England
- Exhibition, Peterloo Gallery, Manchester (solo show)

1972
- President of The Liverpool Academy of Arts
- *I Want* written with Nell Dunn, published by Jonathan Cape
- *America* published by Turret Books
- *I Want*, writers tour with Nell Dunn
- *Henri and Friends in Concert*, tour with Alan Peters, Phil Harrison, Stuart Gordon, Mike Giles, Vivian Stanshall, John Porter and Valerie Movie
- *Recollections*, Liverpool Scene LP released by Charisma
- UK tour with Grimms
- *Autobiography Part I*, BBC Television
- *John Moores Liverpool Exhibition 8*, Walker Art Gallery, Liverpool, 2nd prize winner

1973
- Visiting Lecturer, Bradford Polytechnic
- Meets Carol Ann Duffy
- Writing courses at the Arvon Foundation at Totleigh Barton
- Poet-in-Residence, Lanchester Festival, Coventry
- Reading tour of South West England, West Midlands, North America
- *Autobiography*, recorded (unissued) with music by Alan Peters, Phil Harrison and Stuart Gordon
- *Henri and Friends in Concert*, BBC Radio Merseyside
- *Yesterday's Girl*, play for Granada Television
- Exhibition, *Pen as Pencil*, Brussels
- Exhibition, *Communication*, Walker Art Gallery, Liverpool

1974
- Visiting Lecturer, Bradford Polytechnic
- Poet-in-Residence, Lanchester Festival, Coventry
- *Environments and Happenings*, published by Thames and Hudson
- *The Mersey Sound*, revised edition published by Penguin
- Reading tours of Scotland, Lincolnshire, Germany and Holland
- *The Liverpool Scene*, revival tour with Andy Roberts, Mike Hart, Dave Richards and Mike Kellie
- *Window Event*, Claude Gill Books, Oxford Street, London, to launch *Environments and Happenings*
- *November Dreams* with friends from Bradford Polytechnic Community Arts Department, event for 'Building Sights' series, The Blackie, Great Georges Project, Liverpool
- Exhibition, Richard Demarco Gallery, Edinburgh (with Susan Sterne)
- Exhibition, *Five Realist Painters*, Sunderland Arts Centre
- Exhibition, *Birthday Gardens*, Academy Gallery, Liverpool (solo show)
- *John Moores Liverpool Exhibition 9*, Walker Art Gallery, Liverpool

1975
- Visiting Lecturer in Film and Publications, Bradford Polytechnic, Department of Community Arts
- CNAA Assessor, Wolverhampton and Leeds Polytechnics

- Writing courses for the Arvon Foundation, Lumb Bank
- *The Best of Henri*, published by Jonathan Cape
- Arts Council of Great Britain Writer's Tour of Humberside and North West England
- *Haiku*, published by the Anvil Press, Liverpool
- Birmingham Festival of Performance Art, with Rob Con, Ian Hinchcliffe and Marty St James
- Exhibition, Williamson Art Gallery, Birkenhead (solo show)
- Exhibition, *The Face of Merseyside*, Walker Art Gallery, Liverpool

1976
- Visiting Lecturer, Bradford Polytechnic
- Readings at the Edinburgh Festival with Roger McGough and Brian Patten
- Bicentennial Poetry Tour of the USA
- *One Year*, published by Arc
- *Liverpool Realist Painters* presented by Henri for Arena BBC2
- Exhibition, *Paintings and Drawings, 1960–1976*, Wolverhampton Art Gallery (solo show)
- Exhibition, *Hedges, Gardens and Other Places*, Art Net, London (solo show)

1977
- CNAA Assessor, Wolverhampton and Leeds Polytechnics
- In Rome for Liverpool FC's European Cup Final victory
- *City Hedges: Poems 1970–76* published by Jonathan Cape (cover photographs by Susan Sterne)
- *Beauty & the Beast* with Carol Ann Duffy, published by The Glasshouse Press
- Readings in Holland and at the Edinburgh Festival with Roger McGough and Brian Patten
- *Performance Art*, a programme for BBC Television's Schools Service
- Exhibition, Ibis Gallery, Leamington Spa
- Exhibition, *Peter Moores, Real Life*, Walker Art Gallery, Liverpool
- *100*, centenary exhibition for the Walker Art Gallery, Liverpool
- Exhibition, *Artists of the Wirral*, Williamson Art Gallery, Birkenhead
- Birkenhead Arts Association Purchase Prize

1978
- Visiting Lecturer in Film and Art History, Liverpool Polytechnic
- CNAA Assessor, Leeds Polytechnic
- *Words Without a Story*, published by

Glasshouse Press, with woodcuts by
Frans Masereel
- Readings in Holland and at the Anglo-French
Festival of Spoken Poetry, Paris
- *Henri's Hope Street Poets*, monthly series
of readings, The Everyman Theatre, Liverpool
- *Beauty & the Beast*, performance with
Carol Ann Duffy, Richard Demarco Gallery,
Edinburgh
- *Watchwords*, BBC1 North West with Roger
McGough, Andy Roberts, Julie Walters,
Tony Haygarth and Andrew Schofield
- Exhibition, *Hedges, Debris & Other Places*,
Bootle Art Gallery (solo show)
- Exhibition, *Debris*, Richard Demarco Gallery,
Edinburgh (solo show)
- Exhibition, *Liverpool Nude*, Bluecoat Gallery,
Liverpool
- *John Moores Liverpool Exhibition 11*,
Walker Art Gallery, Liverpool

1979
- Arts Council of Great Britain Writer's Tour
of Lincolnshire and Humberside
- *Un Certain Art Anglais*, Paris (readings)
- *The Big Feller*, musical based on Alfred Jarry's
Ubu Roi (unperformed)
- *The Funeral of Adrian Henri*, performance
with Rob Con and Lol Coxhill, Liverpool Pier
Head and the Academy Gallery, Liverpool
- Milton Keynes Festival, painting and
poetry commission
- Exhibition, Bolton Festival (solo show)
- Exhibition, *Poste Restante*, Liverpool
Academy Gallery

Index
Figure numbers, page numbers

Contributors

Bryan Biggs is Artistic Director of the Bluecoat, Liverpool's centre for the contemporary arts, where in 2011 he curated the exhibition *Democratic Promenade*, which included a section on Adrian Henri's 'total art'. He has written about art and its intersection with popular culture and co-edited several books including *Liverpool City of Radicals, Malcolm Lowry: From the Mersey to the World* and *Art in a City Revisited*. He is also an artist known for his drawings.

Antony Hudek is Curator and Deputy Director, Raven Row, London. From 2012 to 2014 he convened the Exhibition Research Centre, Liverpool John Moores University, which hosted the exhibition that gave rise to this book.

Catherine Marcangeli is a Paris-based art historian and curator. She is a Senior Lecturer at the University of Paris-Diderot, specialising in art since the 1960s. As the executor of the Adrian Henri Estate, she has edited his *Selected and Unpublished Poems, 1965-2000* (Liverpool University Press, 2007), developed the website adrianhenri.com and catalogued his Total Art archive. She has also curated exhibitions of his work in the UK and abroad, including *Adrian Henri – Total Art* at the Exhibition Research Centre, Liverpool John Moores University (2014).

Final page: *Summer Poems without Words*, 1965, ink on paper, 33 × 20 cm

Adrian Henri: Total Artist

Edited by Catherine Marcangeli

With texts by Bryan Biggs, Adrian Henri,
Antony Hudek, Catherine Marcangeli

Published on the occasion of
Adrian Henri: Total Art, an exhibition
curated by Catherine Marcangeli
at the Exhibition Research Centre,
Liverpool John Moores University,
5 July–26 October 2014

Published by Occasional Papers

Copy-edited by Antony Hudek
Designed by Sara De Bondt studio
Typefaces: NN Colroy and Windsor Elongated
Printed by Die Keure
Photographs by Jon Barraclough: pp. 2, 153,
Figs. 1, 11, 21, 31, 39, 43, 44, 49, 56, 58, 59, 60,
66, 69, 80, 84
Photograph by Vesna Bukovcak: p. 152
Photograph by Philip Jones Griffiths: p. 61

Notes on Painting and Poetry by Adrian Henri
(1968) on pp. 108–23 is reprinted from *Tonight
at Noon*, Rapp & Whiting, London 1968

With the support of Liverpool John Moores
University Library Services, the Henry Moore
Foundation, University of Paris Diderot-Sorbonne
Paris Cité

Thanks to Jon Barraclough, Michael Bracewell,
Pete Brown, Rachel Carr, Alex Cox, Juan Cruz,
Fran Disley, Carol Ann Duffy, Mike Evans, Damon
Fairclough, John Gorman, Christopher Gregory,
Liverpool Biennial 2014, Barry Miles, Kate
Morrell, Stephen Pratt, Josie Reed, Andy Roberts,
Dawn Russell, Willy Russell, Jon Savage, Steve
Shepherd, Juliet Shield, Valerie Stevenson

All works and documents part of the Adrian Henri
Archive, Estate of Adrian Henri, Liverpool except
private collections: Figs. 2, 9, 12, 16, 24, 36, 37, 45,
57, 63, and p. 135 (*Batcomposition*)

ISBN: 978-0-9569623-8-6

www.occasionalpapers.org

LIVERPOOL JOHN MOORES UNIVERSITY   Exhibition Research Centre   The Henry Moore Foundation   université PARIS DIDEROT

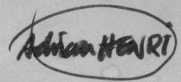

SUMMER POEMS WITHOUT WORDS

(to be done over a period of seven days)

1. Try to imagine your next hangover.

2. Travel on the Woodside ferry with your eyes closed. Travel back with them open.

3. Look for a black cat. Stroke it. This will be either lucky or unlucky.

4. Find a plastic flower. Hold it up to the light.

5. Next time you see someone mowing a lawn smell the smell of freshly-cut grass.

6. Watch 'Coronation Street'. Listen to the 'B' side of the latest Dusty Springfield record.

7. Sit in a city square in sunlight. Remember the first time you made love.

8. Look at every poster you pass next time you're on a bus.

9. Open the works of the world at page 3. Read between the lines.

10. The next time you grit your teeth think about what you're doing.